RIGHT-WING OVERVIEW

The Marketplace and the Bible Join Forces

The Right's Attack on Public Schools

by Barbara Miner

The religious right, helped by more moderate conservative forces, is taking aim at the very concept of public education.

The religious right continues to concentrate on high-profile issues such as restricting reproductive freedom and the rights of gays and lesbians. But make no mistake. Buoyed by the conservative movement's success in gutting welfare and other social programs, the religious right increasingly is targeting its sights on public schools.

It is essential that progressives pay particular attention to the attack on public education, whether or not as individuals they relate directly to public schools. The survival of this country's tradition of public education has far-reaching implications for all who are committed to a democratic society that respects diversity and tolerance. No matter how much this tradition is tarnished and battered in practice, it remains a cornerstone of our democratic vision.

Both the religious right and the broader conservative movement understand that schools play an essential role in instilling society's values in a new generation of people. They know that if they are to reverse the gains of the women's, civil rights, environmental and gay rights movements, they must pay attention to school curriculum and culture.

People for the American Way Foundation, a civil liberties advocacy group based in Washington, D.C., points out that the religious right's education agenda has two main goals:

• To redirect substantial public tax dollars into private, religious schools serving the religious right's core constituency;

• To use whatever public education system remains to impose narrow, Biblically based beliefs on America's next generation.

"After years of refining their tactics, religious right leaders and their political

allies are poised to achieve their plans to redefine and undermine public education in America," notes the 1997 report by People for the American Way, "A Right Wing and a Prayer."

The main political emphasis of the religious right — particularly on a national level — is to implement voucher programs and tax initiatives that use public dollars to help fund religious schools. The beauty of a voucher system, from the religious right's perspective, is that fundamentalist parents would be able to send their children to religious schools controlled by Christian fundamentalists — and have the public pay for it.

Deanna Duby, director of education policy for People for the American Way, notes that national organizations such as The Christian Coalition and Focus on the Family have also put a high priority on affecting local policy for school boards. She points to the enormous amount of material generated by right-wing organizations on how to become involved in

education, including radio programs, books, videos, and training workshops.

The religious right has been increasingly successful in imposing its agenda on public schools. For instance, it successfully pushed to pass federal legislation mandating abstinence-only education. It has also stepped up its censorship of controversial books, particularly those with gay or lesbian themes or those dealing with adolescent sexuality. Further, the religious right has so intimidated some science teachers that they no longer discuss the theory of evolution — considered by scientists to be the cornerstone of modern biology.

An Unholy Alliance

On its own, the religious right does not have the popular support or political clout to implement its agenda. In recent decades, however, it has forged a working relationship with more mainstream conservatives in the Republican Party — an unholy alliance in which each wing of the

Party is trying to use the other for its advantage. The alliance rests on an understanding by both groups that sustaining this coalition is crucial if the Republican Party is to dominate the country's political structures. Thus, even when more moderate conservatives disagree with the religious right (especially on topics such as creationism and a virulent opposition to rights of gay, lesbian and bisexual people), they rarely speak up publicly for fear of jeopardizing the alliance and/or incurring the religious right's wrath.

Periodically, the religious right threatens to bolt from the Republican Party if more mainstream conservatives do not adopt its agenda. As *New York Times* columnist Frank Rich wrote in the summer of 1998, "The religious right now

> *The survival of public education has far-reaching consequences for all who are committed to a democratic society.*

demands an ideological purity that few to the left of the U.S. Taxpayers Party can meet." When threats are made, more mainstream Republicans tend to bow down before the religious right and try to smooth over the differences.

If progressives are to defeat the religious right's agenda, they must scrutinize both the points of unity and the points of difference within the right's attack on the schools, and begin to drive a wedge between the religious right and its allies in

more mainstream conservatism.

Chip Berlet, who has researched the right wing for over 20 years and is currently with the watch-dog group Political Research Associates, argues that progressives must begin to exploit the contradictions with the right. "It's a coalition and like all coalitions, there are points of unity and points of divergence," he told *Rethinking Schools*. "What has allowed them to operate, in part, is that their points of

Religious Group Begins "Exodus 2000"

Leaders of the religious right are waging a campaign to withdraw all "Christian children" from the public schools by the year 2000. The campaign, known as "The Exodus 2000 Project," is being spearheaded with the slogan, "Let My People Go."

The campaign is being organized by some of the top leaders of the religious right, including Dr. D. James Kennedy, pastor of Coral Ridge Presbyterian Church in Florida, and Robert Simonds of Citizens for Excellence in Education.

The idea of an exodus campaign surfaced publicly last February. At that time, Simonds announced "Rescue 2010." Other religious right leaders wanted to move forward the date to the year 2000 — which, perhaps only coincidentally, overlaps with the presidential elections.

The flavor of the campaign is captured in a Sept. 11 press release from E. Ray Moore, director of Exodus 2000. Moore said: "Today some 12-15 million evangelical Christian children, or 90% of the kids from Christian families, are still attending government schools which are totally hostile to their principles and their faith. If these Christian families were to leave Pharaoh's schools for the promised

land of Christian schools or home-schooling, it could trigger the spiritual re-awakening we are all praying and longing for to renew our churches, our nation, and our debased culture. It would seriously cripple the power secularism now holds over our culture by holding our children as near-hostages in state schools."

Moore underscores the importance the religious right attaches to attacking public schools and advocating religiously based instruction by noting, "This is the only battle that counts in the long run, and a battle that can be won, but only if Believers begin the exodus from atheistic public schools."

Reasons for Rescue

Simonds says the main reason Christians should give up on public schools is that "almost all our curriculum bases the instruction unit on a humanist world view, with all its anti-Christian worldly values." He also cites the teaching of evolution and refers to the "sin, homosexuality, the occult, sex and drugs in the public schools." Simonds also opposes state and federal tests, which are deemed a form of government mind control.

The libertarian Separation of School

and State Alliance, meanwhile, argues in its September newsletter that readers should "avoid trying to fix" public schools. Instead, with wording almost identical to press releases from the religious right, it calls upon its supporters to "help rescue children from government schools." It specifically recommends financial contributions to the Children's Scholarship Fund, set up by New York City financier Theodore Forstmann and John Walton of Wal-Mart fame. The Fund provides $1,000 scholarships for low-income families to help pay tuition at private and religious schools; it is designed in part to build support for publicly funded vouchers.

The alliance calls for an end to any government involvement in education, from funding of public schools to compulsory attendance laws. Despite the organization's fringe nature, a number of prominent conservatives have endorsed its goals — such as Ed Crane, president of the Cato Institute, one of the most influential think tanks in Washington, D.C.; Thomas Moore of the equally influential Heritage Foundation; Howard Phillips, head of the U.S. Taxpayer's Party; and U.S. Rep. Ron Paul (R-TX). ■

—Barbara Miner

difference have not been scrutinized sufficiently."

The Key Difference: Religion

From the outside, it often appears that conservatives are of one mind on education: abolish the U.S. Department of Education, return all educational authority to states and localities, and push for school prayer, vouchers, and privatization.

Lamar Alexander.

Phyllis Schlafly.

But their seeming unity masks important differences.

The most significant cleavage is between the religious right, which seeks to place Biblical law at the center of public policy, and those who remain secular in their orientation despite rhetoric that often matches that of the religious right.

"The key difference is in the word religion," argues George Kaplan, an educational analyst in Washington, DC, who has studied the religious right.

(Different terms are used to describe the various forces in the conservative movement: traditional vs. religious right, economic vs. social right, mainstream vs. far right, Old Right vs. New Right. This article generally will refer to the two major groupings as the *religious right* and the more secular *economic right.*)

Kaplan sees a theocratic vision at the heart of the religious right's agenda, in keeping with evangelical Christianity's belief in a literal interpretation of the Bible. For this reason, Christian rightists are obsessed with their children receiving religious instruction as the foundation of their school curriculum. A number of religious-right organizations reflect this parental obsession and place education issues at the center of their political work.

These include Louis Sheldon's Traditional Values Coalition, Rev. Donald Wildmon's American Family Association, Citizens for Excellence in Education/National Association of Christian Educators, Phyllis Schlafly's Eagle Forum, Rev. James Dobson's Focus on the Family, and Pat Robertson's Christian Coalition.

Lee Berg, a Baptist minister who has studied the religious right for over 20 years and now works with the human and civil rights division of the National Education Association (NEA), argues that too many people underestimate the extent to which the religious right is committed to a *theocracy* — a government based on literal interpretation of Biblical principles. Berg points out that many of the top leaders in the religious right have been strongly influenced by Christian Reconstructionism. The movement, in essence, seeks to replace democracy with a theocratic form of government. It argues that secular law is always secondary to biblical law, and that it is the duty of Christians to see that God's law is paramount throughout society. Though the movement has received minimal attention in the mainstream media, some analysts consider it the driving ideology of the leadership of the religious right.

"While the reconstructionists represent only a small minority within Protestant theological circles, they have had tremendous influence on the theocratic right ..." writes Berlet in the book he has edited, *Eyes Right!*. "Reconstructionism is a factor behind the increased violence in the anti-abortion movement, the nastiest of attacks on gays and lesbians, and the new wave of battles over alleged secular humanist influence on the public schools."

The defining text of reconstructionism, *Institutes of Biblical Law*, is an 800-page tome written in 1973 by Rousas John Rushdoony. By providing a theological basis for Christian involvement in politics, it helped spur the growth of the religious right. The flavor of Rushdoony's approach can be captured in this excerpt: "The only true order is founded on Biblical law. All law is religious in nature, and every non-Biblical law-order represents an anti-Christian religion."

While religious conservatives base their ideology on a narrow interpretation of the Bible, economic conservatives pay homage to corporate capitalism and unrestrained markets. Economic conservatives are primarily concerned with increasing the freedom of the market — by cutting taxes, privatizing government services, and reducing government social programs, especially federal programs that redistribute resources and serve the needs of low-income people and people of color.

Progressive educators familiar with the issues argue that the differences between the religious right and the economic right sometimes appear to be based on rhetoric and emphasis — for example, how strongly they push for school prayer or how strongly they attack the rights of gay and lesbian students. Those differences, however, ultimately stem from a fundamental split over the role of religion in education.

Economic conservatives "believe that the free market drives civilization, while the religious right believes that God drives civilization," notes Berlet of Political Research Associates. "Just because God is driving the same way right now as corporate capitalism is a fortunate coincidence for the right."

Common Ground

The religious and economic conservatives try to mask their strategic differences over the role of religion. Thus they are able to join forces on a number of issues. Most important, they both are pushing on the federal and state level for vouchers that would provide tax dollars for private and religious schools. They also support other privatization efforts, such as contracting to for-profit businesses — everything from food service to, in some cases, the entire running of a school.

They both also have an antipathy toward federal education programs, in particular those designed to lessen inequalities due to race, gender, disabilities, or economic status. Both argue that the federal government tilted too far to the advantage of poor people and people of color, and that liberals tilted too far to the left on cultural issues.

Although they publicly downplay anti-unionism as an explicit strategy, econom-

ic and religious conservatives both understand that breaking the power of the teachers unions is essential to cementing Republican control over state and federal education politics. The unions not only are important allies of the Democratic Party, but are one of the few forces in education able to match the financial and organizing resources of the right.

Of the various education issues uniting religious and economic conservatives, vouchers is the most important. Using public dollars to provide vouchers to private schools remains the main political goal of both the religious right and its allies in more mainstream conservatism. A key to defeating the right-wing education agenda of both the religious right and its allies in more mainstream conservatism is to defeat the voucher movement.

The Importance of Vouchers

For religious conservatives, the voucher movement provides a way to funnel public dollars into private Christian schools. For economic conservatives, vouchers serve a number of purposes, including furthering an overall goal of privatizing government services and dismantling social entitlements, as well as undermining the role of government in

providing for the good of all. "To privatize public education is the centerpiece, the grand prize of their overall agenda," Ann Bastian writes in the booklet published by Rethinking Schools in 1996, *Selling Out Our Schools: Vouchers, Markets, and the Future of Public Education.* (See also articles, pages 67 to 77.)

Vouchers also serve an important polit-

William Bennett.

Pat Robertson and Ralph Reed.

ical function for the conservative movement, whether efforts to legislate their use are successful or not. As Bastian writes: "Vouchers unify the different strands of the right: business entrepreneurs looking for a new public carcass to feed on, having used up the Cold War; anti-government libertarians who worship the free market, having noticed that education is the society's largest public institution; social and religious conservatives who want to break down the separation of church and state, while garnering public funds to run their own schools. Many issues divide the right; vouchers unite them and provide an organizing platform."

Politically, vouchers also provide a way to make inroads into the urban Democratic base. Most legislative voucher proposals have targeted low-income students in urban districts and support for vouchers has been stronger among urban African-Americans — who are the group most disserved by the U.S. educational system — than among white Republican suburbanites, who tend, by and large, to be satisfied with their schools.

> *Vouchers serve an important political function for conservatives. Many issues divide various sectors of the Republican Party; vouchers unite them.*

The voucher movement often uses the rhetoric of "school choice," masking its actual goal, which is to promote a system of vouchers to pay for private school attendance. In fact, most voucher proposals don't even use the term "voucher."

Vouchers refer specifically to plans to use public tax dollars to help parents pay tuition at private schools, including religious schools. *School choice*, in contrast, is a much broader concept that also encompasses proposals to let students attend public schools in other districts, or that allows students to choose various public schools within a district.

As of September 1998, the only operating voucher programs were initiatives in Milwaukee and Cleveland. In both cities, conservatives have included religious schools in the programs. Lawsuits have been filed in both cities on grounds that the inclusion of religious schools violates the separation of church and state. Ultimately, the issue is expected to go before the U.S. Supreme Court. (Even if found constitutional, vouchers raise key public policy issues. Should voucher schools, for instance, be considered private schools that can ignore accountability measures that public schools must follow? Will the vouchers schools be able, for instance, to teach that homosexuality is a sin and that creationism is credible science?)

There have been four efforts to institute statewide voucher programs — in Oregon, California, Colorado, and Washington State. All four efforts were put to the voters and defeated by a margin of rough-

The Roots of Right-Wing Differences

Conservatives have traditionally been divided into three main groups: traditional conservatives, neoconservatives, and libertarians. These groups form the core of what is referred to as the economic right.

Traditional conservatives were noted for their opposition to communism and to the New Deal. The neoconservative movement sprang up in the 1960s and 1970s, founded by former "liberals" alarmed by what they considered the excesses of the anti-war, civil rights, and women's movements. These origins explain in part the cultural/social emphasis of many neoconservatives, who are predominantly concerned with social policy, not economic issues.

The neoconservative movement has steadily moved rightward and many people argue it is now indistinguishable from traditional conservatism. Some of the most prominent education reformers, such as Chester Finn, Diane Ravitch, and William Bennett, tend to be associated with the neoconservative movement.

Libertarians tend to be more ideologically driven; they oppose government regulation of the marketplace and champion individual liberty and choice. The libertarians generally support vouchers and privatization based on ideological principle, while other conservatives often support such policies in the belief that private business and private schools will provide services more efficiently and will foster increased "competition." While libertarians are the religious right's most consistent allies in the fight for school vouchers, they are often at odds with the religious right over social concerns such as gay rights and the right to abortion.

(It is important to note that these are ideological differences between the major groups. In practice, many organizations and individuals tend to fudge differences for the sake of political pragmatism.)

The religious right is a relatively new phenomenon in American politics and came to national prominence during the Reagan administration.

During the Reagan era, the religious right was part of a phenomenon known as the New Right, to distinguish it from the traditional or "Old" Right. The New Right combined sophisticated marketing and direct mail techniques with a political message that stressed issues such as "pro-family values" and "busing." By appealing to blue-collar Democrats, the New Right was seen as a crucial ally in realigning American party politics and building the Republican base beyond the country club crowd.

Some of the most well-known religious conservatives from the Reagan presidency have faded, in particular Jerry Falwell and his Moral Majority. But the groups today known as the religious right have their roots in that era. ■

Rev. Lou Sheldon of the Traditional Values Coalition.

The 1995 Conservative Political Action Conference in Washington, DC.

ly 2-1. (One of the unexpected sources of opposition to vouchers came from suburban parents who were not dissatisfied with their schools and who did not want vouchers to be used as a way for urban children to attend suburban schools.) On the federal level, conservatives have tried, to date unsuccessfully, to institute some form of voucher program either through tax measures or so-called "scholarship" programs for low-income students.

Given the difficulties of getting a full-scale voucher program passed, some Republicans are emphasizing tuition tax credits or tax-free savings accounts. Such measures, which are politically appealing because they are packaged as "tax relief," provide a back-handed way for the government to help middle-class parents pay for private schools; while no money is directly given to parents, families are able to reduce the amount of money they would otherwise have to pay in taxes.

Standards

It is easiest to point to various areas where economic and religious conservatives agree on education issues. But if one is to try to drive a wedge into their working coalition, it is important to identify the issues on which they *disagree* — and to publicize those disagreements. The religious right, for instance, often emphasiz-

es an opposition to gay rights, national curriculum standards, and the evils of secular humanism. They support homeschooling, creationism, school prayer, and censorship of what they see as objectionable books. Many of these issues are described in detail elsewhere in this booklet.

One disagreement between the religious right and more mainstream conservatives involves standards, in particular federal standards. More mainstream conservatives have tactically backed away from the issue of federal standards, in part due to pressure from the far right, in part due to the fact that a Democrat now sits in the White House and controls the U.S. Department of Education. But in general, mainstream conservatives have long stressed the need to return to "excellence" and "standards" — which they often use as code words for a curriculum focused on Western civilization and traditional interpretations of history. At this point, the more mainstream right is focusing on instituting state standards — especially in those states where Republicans hold power — as a way to mandate a more conservative and traditional curriculum.

The religious right is opposed to federal standards, even if they are voluntary, on the grounds that they will turn children into objects of government mind control. (Many progressives oppose federal stan-

dards, but on the grounds that they lead to more standardized tests, which have been shown to be biased against poor children and children of color. Progressives also fear that standards are being used to increase tracking and impose a rigid, Eurocentric curriculum.)

As Linda Bowles, a nationally syndicated conservative columnist, wrote in September 1997, "Federal testing will lead to federal control of the curriculum, which opens the door for political ideologues, social change agents, and heathen predators to imprint our children with their messages and agendas." Similar criticisms were launched against the standards-reform known as Outcomes-Based Education (OBE), which was popular earlier in the decade, and the federal initiative Goals 2000, an education reform package first proposed by former President Bush. The far-right attack has been so successful that one never hears the term OBE anymore and rarely hears reference to Goals 2000, even though it technically remains a bi-partisan initiative to improve the nation's schools.

Rote Memorization vs. Thinking

Deanna Duby of People for the American Way notes another critical difference between the two conservative wings: the religious right stresses education based

Impact Visuals/Jennifer Warburg

Paul Weyrich of the Free Congress Foundation.

on rote obedience and memorization; it prefers to provide children ready-made answers instead of encouraging them to think for themselves. This approach is at odds with that of most economic conservatives, who want to see children improve their problem-solving skills and are not necessarily opposed to sexuality education, or drug prevention programs, as long as academic "excellence" is not compromised.

"One of the beliefs that underlies a lot of the religious right's work is that they really don't want any discussion at all about certain issues," Duby said. "They believe that if children are exposed to an idea, or even hear about it, they are vulnerable to being swept up into something different from their parents — that if you hear about sexuality, you are going to have sex, or that if you hear about homosexuality, you are going to become gay."

Media Savvy

One reason that differences between the religious and economic right are sometimes unclear is that the religious right has become media-savvy and has learned to couch its views in high-sounding rhetoric. However, when reading the literature distributed to its members, a different picture emerges.

A typical tract is a book titled *A Guide to the Public Schools for Christian Parents and Teachers and Especially for Pastors*, by Robert Simonds, president of Citizens for Excellence in Education/National Association of Christian Educators. The book notes that there are three ways to educate one's child: home-schooling ("the only truly biblical plan to educate our children"), Christian schooling ("the next best thing"), and public schooling.

Simonds says he understands why parents might use the public school ("the most convenient school"). But he says of public schools: "Morally, children are exposed to many unnecessary courses on human sexuality; occultic New Age indoctrination including necromancy (under hypnosis, talking to the dead); witchcraft; black magic; T.M.; eastern religions, etc. Social and psychological programs, diaries, visiting morgues, writing their own obituaries and grave-stone inscriptions, etc., as English assignments, have duly and rightfully upset parents."

No matter how much the William Bennetts of the world may choose to align with the religious right, it's hard to imagine that they believe such nonsense.

The religious right also masks its true agenda when it is organizing parents at the local level. Thus it is often able to build coalitions of parents and community people who may not agree with the religious-right's overall goals but who are concerned about educational issues raised by the religious conservatives. For instance, well-meaning parents might become involved in a religious-right campaign around curricular issues, such as the teaching of reading — with the religious right demanding an approach that emphasizes only phonics and, unlike the reading philosophy known as whole language, downplays the need to teach young children to understand the content of what they are reading.

The religious right has emphasized both electing fundamentalists to local school boards and training fundamentalist parents and pastors to organize in local schools. No one knows for sure how many religious conservatives serve on the country's 15,000 local school boards, but the number is possibly in the thousands. Sometimes the candidates are openly affiliated with religious fundamentalist organizations; often they are what is known as "stealth" candidates who conceal their true beliefs until elected. As one Christian Coalition member said at a workshop during the coalition's 1995 convention, "We are told not to identify ourselves as Christian Coalition members, just as John Q. Public." Ralph Reed, then executive director of the Christian Coalition, told convention-goers: "I would exchange the Presidency for 2,000 school board seats in the United States."

The religious right has found it particularly useful to use issues of gay rights to attack schools and teachers unions, especially the National Education Association (see articles page 48 to 56).

Conclusion

Despite popular concern about the state of our public schools, there is no indication that the public at large subscribes to the religious right's agenda. Indeed, there remains widespread and deep support for a public system of schools that provide an equal education for all — no matter how tarnished that ideal may be in reality. If the religious right were to win its agenda, that long-standing ideal would be abandoned.

Progressives have the right and responsibility to appeal to the positive American tradition of public schooling. We must defend our system of public schools while at the same time working to transform it so that public schools do indeed provide quality education for all.

Progressives must also push more mainstream conservatives to publicly state: do they support the theocratic vision of the religious right? The right wing will do all it can to mask differences between economic and religious conservatives. It is up to progressives to expose the unholy alliance. ∎

Barbara Miner is managing editor of *Rethinking Schools*. Early versions of this article appeared in *Rethinking Schools*, Spring 1996 (Vol. 10, No. 3) and in *The Public Eye* in the fall/winter of 1997.

The Bell Curve Agenda

*T*he Bell Curve skyrocketed onto best-seller lists in 1994 despite blistering criticism of its view that African Americans, as a group, are less intelligent than whites and that their inferior intelligence is predetermined by genetics. The explosive conclusions of the book, co-authored by Charles Murray and Richard Herrnstein, are generally common knowledge. What is less well-known are the links between the book and educational issues, in particular vouchers.

The Bell Curve's top educational policy recommendation is support for school choice, including public funds for private and religious schools. The book helps explain why some conservatives, despite the rhetoric of choice and equal opportunity, have abandoned public schools and the vision of a quality education for all children.

As the authors of *The Bell Curve* themselves explain on p. 436, "... critics of American education must come to terms with the reality that *in a universal education system, many students will not reach the level of education that most people view as basic*" [emphasis in original].

In general, the book's policy recommendations on elementary and secondary schools call for a shift in thinking away from programs benefitting the "disadvantaged" (who disproportionally are low-income African American) toward the "gifted" (who tend to be affluent whites.)

The Bell Curve was funded in large part by the Milwaukee-based Lynde and Harry Bradley Foundation, considered the country's top financial backer of conservative research, publications, and think tanks. Perhaps not coincidentally, vouchers are the only educational reform consistently and significantly funded by Bradley. In Milwaukee, for instance, the largesse of the Bradley Foundation has been a decisive factor in the development of a voucher program.

Robert Lowe, co-editor of *Selling Out Our Schools: Vouchers, Markets, and the Future of Public Education,* argues, "*The Bell Curve* is a smoking gun. It maintains

that the poor — including the majority of African Americans — are generally incapable of benefiting from education ... The link between *The Bell Curve* and the Bradley Foundation strongly suggests that the interest of the foundation ... is the diversion of resources spent on urban schools, whose students are largely deemed uneducable, to the allegedly worthy children of more affluent families."

C.J. Prentiss, an African-American legislator in Ohio, notes that voucher advocates have tried to win converts by arguing that vouchers will improve opportunities for the poor. "You have to be suspicious," she says, "of someone who argues that on the one hand, African Americans are dumber than whites, and then, on the other, comes into the Black community and says, 'We are going to make you as bright as you can be, here are some vouchers. ... I believe vouchers are simply a way to dismantle public schools and use tax dollars to fund an elitist private school system. But voucher advocates know it would be suicide to say that openly."

Same Results

Charlie Dee, an instructor at the Milwaukee Area Technical College who has been active in the struggle against vouchers, also underscores the ideological links between vouchers and the conclusions of *The Bell Curve.* "The prescriptions that flow from *The Bell Curve* and the impact of a voucher system would have the same result," he says. "Both would exacerbate class and racial disparity in our society and in our educational system."

The Bell Curve, the Bradley Foundation, and conservative policy-makers share a broader ideological per-

spective that posits that the social problems facing this country are not related to structural issues of poverty, wage disparities, racism and discrimination, but rest in the behavior and abilities of individuals. Lowe argues that *The Bell Curve* makes clear is that "the agenda is not so much to get the government off the backs of the people, but to get the redistributive government off the backs of the well-to-do. And by redistributive I mean those aspects of the government that call upon the well-to-do to help provide social services to the less fortunate."

Murray, meanwhile, has not been daunted by the criticism of *The Bell Curve.* In an interview with *The National Review* in December 1997, he repeated his views that many students are incapable of rising above minimal educational standards. He particularly criticized President Clinton's call for two years of college for everyone, noting that "universal college education cannot be. Most people are not smart enough to profit from an authentic education."

Murray also said that the book has had significant impact on policy issues, although few are willing to say so openly. He called *The Bell Curve* "the stealth public-policy book of the 1990s. It has created a subtext on a range of issues. Everybody knows what the subtext is. Nobody says it out loud." ∎

— Barbara Miner

THE BELL CURVE... HAS A FAMILIAR RING TO IT.

Economic Conservatives and Religious/Far Right Organizations

The following four pages list major organizations generally affiliated with the economic and the religious/far right wings of the Republican Party. The categories are in line with the organization's major orientation, and the groups often overlap on specific policies. The term "economic" is used to encompass a broad grouping of libertarians, entrepreneurs, free-market ideologues, so-called "moderate" Republicans, and cultural conservatives. "Religious/far right" refers to those Christian-based groups such as the Christian Coalition and far-right allies such as the Free Congress Foundation.

ECONOMIC CONSERVATIVES

Economic think tanks/ policy groups

The following are some of the main think tanks and public policy groups based primarily on a free-market, economic orientation. Although they do not receive the same publicity as the religious right, these organizations unquestionably rival its power.

Educationally, they focus on vouchers, charters, deregulation, privatization, and oppose federal programs designed to further equity, such as bilingual education, special education, and Title 1. While some stress cultural issues, they tend to shy away from concerns such as prayer in the schools.

American Enterprise Institute
Founded in 1943 to promote free-enterprise economics and to oppose policies of the New Deal, AEI is often considered the most powerful conservative think tank after the Heritage Foundation. *The Bell Curve* was co-authored by AEI fellow Charles Murray.
Contact: 1150 17th St., NW, Washington, DC 20036. 202-862-5800.

Cato Institute
Libertarian oriented, Cato was founded in the 1970s by Ed Crane, a former head of the Libertarian Party. A strong supporter of vouchers and privatization, it also supports gay rights, decriminalization of drugs and relaxed immigration controls.
Contact: 1000 Massachusetts Ave., NW, Washington, DC 20001. 202-842-0200. Internet: www.cato.org.

Center for Education Reform
A relatively new organization, the center is increasingly active in mainstream debates and is headed by Jeanne Allen, a former policy analyst for the Heritage Foundation. Its emphases include vouchers and privatization. It helped form the Education Leaders Council, a grouping of conservative school board chiefs and state school board members.
Contact: 1001 Connecticut Ave., NW, Suite 204, Washington, DC 20036. 800-521-2118. E-mail: cerdc@aol.com. Internet: www.edreform.com.

Center for the Study of Popular Culture
Founded in 1988 by former leftists David Horowitz and Peter Collier, the center is the pit-bull of right-wing think tanks. It focuses on cultural issues and led the attack on the Corporation for Public Broadcasting and the National Endowments for the Arts and Humanities. Its monthly tabloid *Heterodoxy* has the appearance of a sophomoric college newspaper and focuses on "political correctness" controversies. Its tabloid *The Report Card* zeroes in on K-12 education and mercilessly attacks everything from teachers unions to whole language, and promotes anything to do with vouchers.
Contact: PO Box 67398, Los Angeles, CA 90067. 800-752-6562.

The Educational Excellence Network
A project of the Hudson Institute, the network was founded in 1982 by Chester E. Finn, Jr. and Diane S. Ravitch. The network emphasizes privatization, vouchers, charters, standards, and a core curriculum centered on Western Civilization. Formerly associated with the Hudson Institute, the network is now a project of the Thomas B. Fordham Foundation in Washington, DC.
Contact: The Thomas B. Fordham Foundation, 1015 18th St. NW, Suite 300. Washington, DC 20036. 202-223-5450. Internet: www.edexcellence.net.

Empower America
Founded in 1993 by William Bennett and Jack Kemp, it bridges economic issues such as a flat tax proposal with cultural issues popular with social conservatives; it also strongly supports school vouchers.
Contact: 1776 "I" St., NW, Suite 890, Washington, DC 20006. 202-452-8200. Internet: www.empower.org.

Heritage Foundation
Founded in 1973, Heritage is the most powerful conservative think tank in the country and is sometimes considered a shadow government. It concentrates on economic issues, but acts as an important bridge to social conservatives through a secondary focus on cultural issues. Educationally, its emphasis is on privatization, vouchers, eliminating federal programs and the U.S. Department of Education, and lower taxes. It tends to ignore and/or downplay issues such as school prayer and sex education. Its web page is a gold-mine of information.
Contact: 214 Massachusetts Ave., NE, Washington, DC 20002. 202-546-4400. E-mail: Insider@heritage.org. Internet: www.heritage.org.

Hoover Institution

Hoover began as the Hoover War Library in 1919 and became independent of Stanford University in 1959. It is the oldest and most influential of conservative think tanks based on college or university campuses. Hoover's focus is on promoting "free markets and free societies," and it has vigorously pushed privatization and vouchers. Its research fellows include Thomas Sowell, an economist who writes frequently on education issues, economist Milton Friedman, and Terry Moe, co-author of the pro-voucher book, *Politics, Markets, and America's Schools.* Ronald Reagan and Margaret Thatcher are honorary fellows.

Contact: Stanford University, Stanford, CA 94305. 650-723-1754. Internet: www.hoover.stanford.edu.

The Hudson Institute

Founded in 1961, the institute was the brainchild of the late Herman Kahn and for many years focused on national security and international affairs. It now also has a strong emphasis on domestic issues, including education. Its trustees include Dan Quayle, vide president during the Bush administration.

Contact: PO Box 26-919, Indianapolis, IN 46226. 317-545-1000. Internet: www.hudson.org/hudson.

Manhattan Institute

This New York City think tank has been generally associated with the Reagan right since its founding in 1978, but is perceived by some as less ideologically rigid than many conservative think tanks. It is perhaps best known as the home of Charles Murray when he wrote his attack on welfare, *Losing Ground.* (The institute asked Murray to leave when he began researching material for *The Bell Curve.*) The institute sponsors the Center for Educational Innovation and works on restructuring public schools within a free-market framework. It publishes *City Journal,* an urban affairs quarterly.

Contact: 52 Vanderbilt Ave., New York, NY 10017. 212-599-7000.

Reason Foundation

A libertarian-oriented think tank founded in 1978, Reason is the leading national advocate of the privatization of government services. It publishes *Reason* magazine and a monthly newsletter, *Privatization Watch.*

Contact: 3415 S. Sepulveda Blvd., Suite 400, Los Angeles, CA 90034. 310-391-2245.

The Separation of School & State Alliance

Founded by Marshall Fritz, the alliance is an ultra-libertarian organization calling for an end of public support of schools. It opposes compulsory attendance laws and use of tax dollars to fund schools, and advocates home schooling.

Contact: 4578 N. First #310, Fresno, CA 93726. 209-292-1776. Internet address: www.sepschool.org.

Legal Groups

Institute for Justice

Especially active on school vouchers, this Washington-based group is helping to defend the Wisconsin legislation that seeks to provide tax dollars for religious schools. Its litigation director, Clint Bolick, is best known outside education circles for spearheading the attack on Clinton nominee Lani Guinier.

Landmark Legal Foundation

Based in Kansas City, MO, Landmark is a national firm founded in 1976 to advance a free market economy. It is also defending the Wisconsin voucher legislation.

RELIGIOUS/FAR RIGHT GROUPS

The following national organizations are associated with the religious/far right. Some, such as the Free Congress Foundation, are not necessarily religiously based but embrace much of the religious right agenda. (Special thanks to People for the American Way and the Institute for First Amendment Studies for their information.)

National Organizations

American Family Association

Founded in 1977 as the National Federation for Decency by Rev. Donald E. Wildmon. A Christian-based organization, its empire includes publications, radio programs, and state chapters. In 1993 its annual income was about $6 million. It claims to have 1.7 to 1.8 million members, although a recent *Newsweek* article put the figure at 400,000 in 1995. It publishes the monthly *AFA Journal,* with a circulation of nearly 500,000, and its 30-minute radio show is broadcast on about 1,200 local radio stations. With a budget of over $10 million, it has about 40 employees. Wildmon was also a national co-chair of the Buchanan for President campaign in 1996.
Contact: PO Drawer 2440, Tupelo, MS 38803. 601-844-5036. Internet address: www.afa.net.

Council for National Policy

Founded in 1981, the council is a highly secretive umbrella organization of more than 500 far-right leaders. Its membership roster is a virtual who's who of the far right and includes national legislative leaders such as Rep. Tom DeLay (R-TX) and Sens. Jesse Helms (R-NC) and Lauch Faircloth (R-NC), and organizational leaders such as Ralph Reed, Pat Robertson, Paul Weyrich and Gary Bauer. Membership is $1,500 a year, plus $300 for its newsletter.

Chalcedon

Founded in 1964, it is often considered the leading think-tank of the religious right. Its chairman, Rousas John Rushdoony, is seen as the father of Christian Reconstructionism, an influential doctrine which mandates a return to Biblical law and the creation of Christ's Kingdom on earth. Rushdoony supports the concept of a theocracy and has criticized democracy and pluralism because "the believer is asked to associate on a common level of total acceptance with the atheist, the pervert, the criminal, and the adherents of other religions."
Contact: PO Box 158, Vallecito, CA 95251. 209-736-4365.

Christian Coalition

Founded in 1989 out of the ashes of the Moral Majority, it is one of the most powerful of the religious right organizations. It has two main goals: take working control of the Republican Party by working from the grassroots up, and electing "Christian candidates" to public office. The chairman of the board is Pat Robertson, but the man most credited with its growth is Ralph Reed Jr., a young, savvy political operator who is now an independent consultant for Republican candidates. Robertson's views are carried daily on his *700 Club* cable show, which reaches about 7 million viewers a week. The Christian Coalition has also formed a subsidiary, the Catholic Alliance.
Contact: PO Box 1990, Chesapeake, VA 23320. 757-424-2630. Internet address: www.cc.org.

Citizens for Excellence in Education/ National Association of Christian Educators

Founded in 1983, the CEE/NACE is one of the most active religious right groups on education. Rev. Robert Simons claims that between 1989 and 1994, his group helped elect 12,000 conservative Christians to school boards nationwide. It publishes the bimonthly *Education Newsline* and has promoted its booklet, *How to Elect Christians to Public Office.*
Contact: PO Box 3200, Costa Mesa, CA 92628. 949-251-9333.

Concerned Women For America

Founded in 1979 and led by Beverly La-Haye, Concerned Women is one of the most virulently anti-gay, anti-sex education groups in the country. It also opposes anti-drug and alcohol abuse programs that emphasize self-esteem. Its 30-minute daily radio show reaches hundreds of thousands of people. It publishes the monthly *Family Voice,* and the monthly *Issues at a Glance.* It also publishes a newsletter specifically for churches, *Family Watch,* which is distributed to about 500,000 people.
Contact: 1015 15th St., NW, Washington, DC 20005. 202-488-7000.

Eagle Forum

Founded in 1972, the forum is led by Phyllis Schlafly, who is most well known for her successful fight against the Equal Rights Amendment in the 1970s. A national leader in the fight against OBE, Goals 2000, and sex education, the Eagle Forum has recently focused on homophobic issues. It publishes a monthly *Education Reporter* and books such as *Child Abuse in the Classroom,* which "explains what has happened to the public schools of America." Schlafly also has a syndicated column that appears in newspapers across the country.
Contact: PO Box 618, Alton, Il. 62002. 618-462-5415. Internet address: www.eagleforum.org. The Forum also has a separate Education Center at 7800 Bonhomme, St. Louis, MO 63105. 314-721-1213.

Family Research Council

Founded in 1981, the council merged with Focus on the Family from 1988-1992, then became independent again. Its president is Gary Bauer, who has emerged as a key religious right leader and Republican operative. Bauer is the former chairman of the Citizens Committee to

firm Clarence Thomas and during the Reagan administration was a policy analyst and an undersecretary in the Department of Education. The council publishes a weekly fax report on education and the bi-monthly *Family Policy,* maintains a legislative hotline, has a weekly television show, *Straight Talk,* a daily radio commentary called Washington Watch, and a newsletter by the same name.
Contact: 801 G St., NW, Washington, DC 20001. 800-225-4008; Legislative Hotline: 202-783-HOME. Internet address: www.frc.org.

Focus on the Family
Founded in 1977, it is led by James Dobson. A virtual media empire, it publishes the monthlies *Focus on the Family, Citizen, Plugged In,* and *Clubhouse* and *Clubhouse Jr.* magazines. Its radio broadcasts reach an estimated 3-5 million people in the U.S., and 3,000 stations in other countries. It claims a membership of 2.1 million members.
Contact: Focus on the Family, Colorado Springs, CO 80995. 719-531-3400. Internet: www.family.org.

Free Congress Foundation
Founded in 1977, the foundation is headed by Paul Weyrich, one of the most influential leaders of the far right. Weyrich is the founding president of the Heritage Foundation, the man who suggested the term "moral majority" to Jerry Falwell and who suggested that Pat Robertson enter politics. Free Congress is aggressively active at the grass-roots level on a broad range of social issues, not just education.
Contact: 717 Second St., NE, Washington, DC 20002. 202-546-3000. E-mail: kmackey@fcref.org. Internet address: www.freecongress.org.

Home School Legal Defense Association
The association is headed by Michael Farris, formerly with Moral Majority and former education advisor for Pat Buchanan during the 1996 presidential campaign. The association provides legal information and, if necessary, representation for home-schooling issues. Other services include the National Center for Home

Educators and the bi-monthly *Home School Court Report.*
Contact: PO Box 3000, Purcellville, VA 20134. 540-338-5600; fax: 504-338-2733.

Traditional Values Coalition
One of the more stridently homophobic of the religious right organizations, the coalition was founded in 1981 and is led by the Rev. Louis Sheldon. A typical fund-raising brochure will proclaim in bold letters, "Yes, Lou, STOP Clinton's homosexual rampage." The group claims connections to 31,000 churches and has active chapters in 20 states. It publishes *Traditional Values Report,* a bi-monthly newsletter, and produces videos such as *Gay Rights/Special Rights,* and *The Big Lie,* which claims to show how framers of the U.S. Constitution did not advocate the separation of church and state.
Contact: 100 S. Anaheim Blvd., Suite 350, Anaheim, CA 92805. 714-520-0300. Washington office: 139 "C" St. SE, Washington, DC 20003. 202-547-8570.

There are also a number of other national policy groups affiliated with the right that, while they may not focus on education issues, generally support the far-right perspective. These include:

National Rifle Association
(Richard D. Riley, President);

National Right to Life Committee
(Wanda Franz, MD, President);

National Right to Work Committee
(Reed Larson, President);

U.S. Taxpayers Party
(Howard Phillips, President);

Operation Rescue (Terry Randall).

Legal Groups

While many religious groups maintain their own legal arms, there are three key legal groups affiliated with the religious right.

Alliance Defense Fund
Founded by leaders of the religious right such as James Dobson of Focus on the Family and Don Wildmon of the American Family Association, the fund is dedicated to "Reclaiming legal ground for the body of Christ." The ADF does not litigate, but finances the training and preparation of attorneys. Based in Phoenix, AZ.

Rutherford Institute
Founded in 1982 by John Whitehead, it is a Christian-based legal group that has been linked to the extremist views of Christian Reconstructionism, which seeks to establish a theocracy. It also publishes a monthly magazine. In 1994 it had an annual budget of about $11 million and 9 staff attorneys. Based in Charlottesville, VA.

American Center for Law & Justice
Affiliated with Pat Roberston and concentrating on religious liberty cases. Along with Rutherford, it is the pre-eminent religious right legal arm. Based in Virginia Beach, VA. ■

Progressive Groups Monitoring the Right Wing

There are a number of liberal and progressive organizations monitoring the right, in particular the religious/far right. They include:

Americans for Religious Liberty
Has extensive publications on the religious right and on issues such as vouchers. *Contact:* Box 6656, Silver Spring, MD 20916. 301-598-2447.

Americans United For Separation of Church and State
Focuses on First Amendment issues, in particular on the voucher movement. *Contact:* 1816 Jefferson Place, NW, Washington, DC 20036. 202-466-3234.

Anti-Defamation League of B'nai B'rith
Established in 1913, the league combats not only anti-Semitism but bigotry and racism. It was one of the first organizations to warn of the growing power of armed, right-wing militias. *Contact:* 823 United Nations Plaza, New York, NY 10017. 212-490-2525.

Center for Democratic Renewal
Based in Atlanta, the center has a particular focus on racist, far-right groups such as militias and white supremacist organizations. It increasingly is also focusing on countering right-wing rhetoric and policy initiatives in general. Extensive publications. *Contact:* PO Box 50469, Atlanta, GA 30302. 404-221-0025. E-mail: cdr@igc.apc.org

Fairness and Accuracy in Reporting
This media watch-dog publishes a bi-monthly newsletter and focuses on right-wing media influence. It has a wide range of resources and publications. *Contact:* 130 W. 25th St., New York, NY 10001. 212-633-6700; fax 212-727-7668. Internet: www.fair@fair.org.

Institute for First Amendment Studies
Founded in 1984, the institute publishes the monthly *Freedom Writer Magazine,* which not only reports on the far right but offers advice on counter-organizing. Its vice-president, Skip Porteus, reportedly has moles in a number of far right organizations. *Contact:* PO Box 589, Great Barrington, MA 02130. 413-274-0012. E-mail: ifas@berkshire.net. Internet: www.ifas.org.

National Abortion and Reproductive Rights Action League (NARAL)
Publishers of *Sexuality Education in America: A State-By-State Review, 1995.* The study is the first comprehensive national survey of sex education laws. $15 suggested donation. *Contact:* NARAL Legal Department, 202-973-3017, or write to NARAL, 1156 15th St., NW, Washington, DC 20005.

National Center for Science Education
Founded in 1983, NCSE has a quarterly newsletter, a biannual journal, and various pamphlets to improve and support the teaching of evolution in public schools. It is affiliated with the American Association for the Advancement of Science and the National Science Teachers Association. *Contact:* PO Box 9477, Berkeley, CA 94709. 510-526-1674.

National Coalition Against Censorship
The coalition publishes a newsletter and organizes against censorship. Members range from the ACLU to the National Council for Social Studies, the Newspaper Guild, Union of American Jewish Congregations, and the American Library Association. *Contact:* 275 Seventh Ave., New York, NY 10001. 212-807-6222.

National Education Association, Human and Civil Rights Division
The division's Freedom to Teach and Learn Project monitors the religious right's attacks on public education. Provides resources and strategies for responding to the religious right. *Contact:* NEA-HCR, 1201 16th St. NW, Washington, DC 20036. 202-822-7700.

National Gay & Lesbian Task Force
The NGLTF organizes at the regional and national levels and publishes the *Fight the Right Action Kit. Contact:* 2320 17th St., NW, Washington, DC 20009. 202-332-6483.

People for the American Way
Probably the best single source of information on the religious right, People for the American Way publishes a variety of publications and reports. Especially useful is its 70-page booklet, *An Activists Guide to Protecting the Freedom to Learn.* Its web page is also particularly useful. *Contact:* 2000 "M" St., NW, Suite 400, Washington, DC 20036. 202-467-4999. E-mail: pfaw@pfaw.org. Internet: www.pfaw.org.

Political Research Associates
Founded in 1981, this group provides research and analysis on the far right, electronically and in printed form. It maintains a free Bulletin Board System that can be accessed by dialing 781-221-5815 with a modem. *Contact:* 120 Beacon St., 3rd Floor, Somerville, MA 02143. 718-661-9313. To contact PRA via E-mail: publiceye@igc.apc.org. Internet address: www.publiceye.org/pra.

Sexuality Information and Education Council of the U. S. (SIECUS)
Publishes a "Community Action Kit" that provides information on effective and accurate sexuality education and that helps counter the radical right's campaign against sexuality education. ($19.95, including s&h.) *Contact:* SIECUS, 130 West 42nd Street, Suite 350, New York, NY 10036. 212-819-9770.

Southern Poverty Law Center, Klanwatch/Militia Task Force
Klanwatch and the Militia Task Force monitor white supremacist groups and the anti-government Patriot Movement. The Southern Poverty Law Center also sponsors the education magazine *Teaching Tolerance. Contact:* 400 Washington Ave., Montgomery, AL 36104. 334-264-0286. ∎

CENSORSHIP

When Good Books Can Get Schools in Trouble

Reading, Writing, and Censorship

by Barbara Miner

*A*nnie On My Mind is an award-winning novel about two young women who meet at New York's Metropolitan Museum of Art, fall in love, and struggle with declaring their homosexuality to family and friends. The book had been in the high school libraries in Olathe, KS, without incident since the early 1980s.

Until Dec. 13, 1993. On that day, Olathe superintendent Ron Wimmer unilaterally ordered the book removed from the high school library.

Wimmer said he made his decision in order to "avoid controversy." In preceding months, *Annie On My Mind* had been the target of protests by religious fundamentalists and the book had been burned on the steps outside the Kansas City School District offices. Wimmer's action did anything but avoid controversy, however. Student petitions calling for the book's reinstatement, rancorous public hearings, and a lawsuit ensued. The School Board in Olathe, a city of 64,000 people 25 miles south of Kansas City, MO, backed Wimmer's decision. It argued that the schools had a legitimate pedagogical right to teach students that homosexuality is wrong.

Almost two years later, on Nov. 29, 1995, the matter was settled when Federal Judge G. Thomas Van Bebber ruled that the book was removed because the board and superintendent "disagreed with ideas expressed in the book," not because the book lacked educational merit. Van Bebber ruled that the banning was an unconstitutional attempt to "prescribe what shall be orthodox in politics, nationalism, religion, or other matters of opinion."

Few challenges to books in our public schools are quite so dramatic. But the controversy over *Annie On My Mind* nonetheless highlights a reality facing teachers and school districts across the country. Censorship is alive and well. Further, it is sometimes part of a larger campaign by

conservative or religious fundamentalist groups to impose their particular curriculum focus on public schools and to build support for public school alternatives such as vouchers.

"[T]he urge to censor is hardly the monopoly of any political group," notes the American Civil Liberties Union. "But the greatest threat today comes from the fundamentalist right, with its ideological hostility to other religious or philosophical systems, to homosexuality, to sex education, and indeed to the basic idea of secular education."

As with any issue, however, scratch beneath the surface and complexities emerge. Only the minority of censorship controversies are as clear cut as Olathe's attempt to censor *Annie On My Mind.*

How, for example, are teachers to distinguish between censorship attempts and legitimate parental concerns over a particular book's appropriateness? What distinctions might be made between complaints about a required book in a required class versus an optional book in an elective class, or calls to ban a book from the school library? Are complaints about curricula potentially grounded in a larger problem of poor relations between a teacher and parents?

Teachers must also address the issue of self-censorship. If certain books are avoided because they are controversial, how does that undercut what should be one of the central purposes of education — to help students learn to critically evaluate and make informed decisions about controversial issues so they can become full participants in this country's civic and political life?

"The health of a democracy is not so much about how people agree but how they choose to disagree," argues Don Ernst, director of government relations at the Association for the Supervision of Curriculum and Development (ASCD) and the group's point person on censorship. "Students need to have the skills, the abilities to critique and analyze a wide array of viewpoints."

Censorship in school primarily involve issues of curriculum and library materials. Other dimensions of censorship include student speech, teacher speech (particularly around issues of foreign policy and issues of sexual orientation) and, increasingly, the Internet.

There are no hard and fast rules about which books may be targeted. Potentially controversial books range from William Faulkner's *As I Lay Dying* for its profanity, to Richard Wright's *Native Son* because it contains the word "nigger," to Bruce Coville's book *My Teacher Glows in the Dark* because it includes the words "armpit farts" and "farting" (see article page 26). *Where's Waldo* was pulled from the Springs Public School library on Long

Island because there was a picture of a naked breast on one page — even though, as former *New York Times* columnist Anna Quindlen wrote, the breast was "the size of the last letter in this sentence." In the Baltimore County school libraries, Kevin O'Malley's *Frog Went A-Courtin'* was placed in a restricted area because of Froggy's nefarious activities, including burning money and speeding away from the cat police. In West Virginia, in November 1997, the Jackson County School Board pulled 16 books from school libraries including Alice Walker's *The Color Purple*, *100 Q&A about AIDS*, and Tom Clancy's *The Hunt for Red October*.

The prime targets for censorship are books that mention sex, talk about sex education, or deal with gay and lesbian issues. Books are also likely to come under attack if they contain profane language or violence, are seen as condoning "New Age" philosophies such as meditation, are deemed "too scary" for little kids, or don't teach "proper respect for authority."

Rarely do those challenging books use the word censorship. "Nobody wants to call himself or herself a censor," notes Mark I. West, professor of English at the University of North Carolina and author of *Trust Your Children: Voices Against Censorship in Children's Literature.* "Everybody says they are protecting children, or they are defending against blasphemy, or defending family values."

What is Censorship?

The American Association of School Administrators (AASA), in the book *Censorship and Selection: Issues and Answers for Schools*, defines censorship as: "[T]he removal, suppression, or restricted circulation of literary, artistic, or educational materials — of images, ideas, and information — on the grounds that these are morally or otherwise objectionable in light of standards applied by the censor." The book, published jointly with the American Library Association (ALA), distinguishes between censorship and the ongoing, necessary reality of selecting educationally appropriate materials for the curriculum and school library. As a rule of thumb, the AASA book argues,

censorship rests on an exclusion of materials, while selection involves an inclusion of materials "carried out by trained professionals, familiar with the wide variety of available choices and guided by a clear grasp of the educational purposes to be fulfilled."

There are generally three levels of challenges to school materials, according to Deanna Duby, director of education policy for People for the American Way, a Washington D.C.-based organization opposed to censorship and other attacks on the freedom to learn in public schools.

• A parent who doesn't want their child to read a particular book.

• A parent, teacher, administrator, or school board member who argues that no one in the class or school should read the book in dispute.

• Someone who is part of an organized

campaign, whether of a local or national group, and who goes in ready for a fight and wants to make a broader political point.

The first type of challenge is often worked out at the classroom level when a teacher explains the curricular purpose of a book or how a book with profane language can still have educational merit, or offers an alternative reading assignment to a student. While there is a tendency to sometimes lump together censorship and challenges to books, teachers need to understand that any parent has the right to question the educational appropriateness of a particular book. The Bill of Rights protects not only freedom of speech but the right to petition the government for redress of grievances — and public school teachers are government employees.

Most experts on censorship argue that the line is crossed when the parent demands that no one in the class, or in the entire school, should read the book or material being challenged. Bannings spawned by an individual parent's complaint seem to be the most common form of censorship, according to groups that track the issue.

Censorship is alive and well in U.S. schools. But rarely do those who challenge books use the word censorship. Instead, they argue that they are protecting children from "inappropriate" materials or are "defending family values."

"One of our recommendations is that if a parent or student objects to a particular book that is being read by the entire class, the student be given an alternative book," says Charles Suhor, a representative of the National Council of Teachers of English (NCTE), who often deals with censorship issues. "If the parent still objects, they are in the position of saying they want to not only guide their child's reading but the reading of other students. And that, we think, is censorship."

While so-called opt-out provisions are

not without their problems, they have provided an important safety valve that "defuses the ability of a parent or group to censor books," argues West. Coming up with alternative assignments can be disruptive to the curriculum and a "bit of a headache" for teachers, West notes, "but a lot less of a headache than spending your afternoons and evenings at a school board meeting justifying why you are assigning a particular book."

The clearest cases of censorship involve demands to remove an existing book from the library. Cindy Robinson, associate director of the Office for Intellectual Freedom at the American Library Association, notes that there are sometimes different issues involved in challenges to materials in the curriculum versus materials in the school library. "When you are dealing with issues in the curriculum, there are questions of whether the material is appropriate to the grade level, to the subject matter, and so forth," she says. "Whereas in the library, you are talking about voluntary reading and the need for a wide variety of materials so you can fulfill the needs of all children in the school."

Organized Campaigns

The most explosive controversies, even if not the most common, involve complaints that are part of an organized campaign. Most of these broader attacks are launched by organizations or individuals affiliated with what is commonly called the religious right — religious fundamentalist groups which advocate a literal interpretation of the Bible and which organize politically to impose their religious perspective on public institutions. Some of the most active religious right organizations involved in school censorship issues are the Eagle Forum, Concerned Women for America, Focus on the Family, The Family Research Council, the American Family Association, and Citizens for Excellence in Education.

One way for teachers to distinguish between legitimate parental concerns and organized campaigns is to look for patterns. Are objections from individual parents worded the same? Are other teachers getting similarly worded complaints?

"That's a pretty good tip-off that the objections may be orchestrated," says West. "It's slightly alarming when that happens because those kind of complaints rarely resolve themselves at the teacher level. They almost always end up at the administration or school board level."

The religious right's influence also goes beyond concerted campaigns. Often, challenges may come from individuals who merely listen to television or radio broadcasts or receive mailings from religious right organizations. "It's not that people are meeting in secret," notes Kate Frankfurt, director of advocacy for the Gay and Lesbian Education Network. "It's just

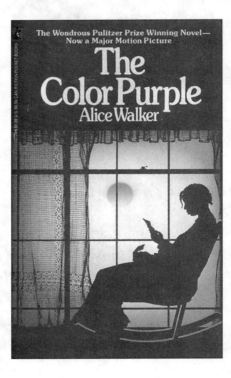

The Wondrous Pulitzer Prize Winning Novel—
Now a Major Motion Picture

The Color Purple
Alice Walker

that the right is very organized in terms of speaking to their members and the broader public, sending out mailings with a call to action, and fanning the flames of misinformation and fears."

In recent years, the religious right has moved beyond censorship of particular books and is now "much more concerned with broader issues, arguing, for instance, that they don't want sex education, or multicultural issues, or anything mentioning gay issues," according to Duby of People for the American Way. In addition to opposing existing books in the curricu-

lum, the religious right is also trying to get their own material in, such as books advocating creationism or an abstinence-only approach to sex education.

Two of the religious right's main emphases are attacking broad-based sex education curriculum and materials dealing with gay and lesbian issues. Concerned Women for America (CWA), which says it has about 500,000 members and is the largest women's organization in the country, for years has attacked the National Education Association for its support of "pro-homosexual propaganda." The CWA also distributes materials such as its leaflet entitled, "Six Action Steps You Can Take To Oppose the Homosexual Agenda in Your Community's Schools."

One of CWA's current campaigns targets the video "It's Elementary: Talking About Gay and Lesbian Issues in School." The documentary, which is intended as a resource for teachers and PTAs, looks at how different schools have worked to develop a more inclusive anti-bias curriculum that examines stereotypes and intolerance toward gay and lesbian people.

In an August 1997 fund-raising letter, CWA calls the film "an aggressive new national campaign to put an extremely dangerous pro-homosexual video in every school in America to be viewed by children as young as kindergarten age." The letter goes on to argue that the video is "being used to guide schoolchildren into ungodly and immoral behavior that leads to death."

Community Standards

In their pronouncements before the general public or the mainstream media, religious right organizations usually tone down their rhetoric. Two of their most common arguments are that a book "violates community standards" and/or is not "age appropriate." Both concepts are important parts of the discussion but are often misused by groups or people attempting to unconstitutionally impose their particular political or religious viewpoint on schools.

Perhaps the best safeguard is to make sure that schools and districts have developed policies which underscore the importance of providing students with a wide range of materials, and which outline how materials are selected. It is also essential that challenges deal with the specifics of the book or materials in question. The vaguer the complaint and the more general the appeal to "community standards," the more the issue will be prone to political manipulation rather than being decided on its educational merit.

Chanting a mantra of "community standards" begs the question of who defines community and how they do so. Does something in the curriculum violate the standards of the Black community? The white community? The gay and lesbian community? The parent community? The tax-paying community? The school community? Further, appeals to community standards and majority rule cannot be used to circumvent constitutional concerns over freedom of speech (see page 27 for an article on U.S. Supreme Court rulings on censorship and schools).

"Our system is built on two pillars, democracy and liberty," notes Loren Siegel, director of public education for the American Civil Liberties Union. "The democracy part pertains to the concept of majority rule on issues such as elections, passage of legislation, and so forth. The liberty part pertains to restrictions on majority rule and the protections of minorities, whether they are racial minorities, religious minorities, or political minorities."

There are certain inalienable rights that are given to every person in the United States by virtue of the Bill of Rights, such as freedom of speech, freedom of religion, and the right to due process, Siegel underscores. "Those are not up for grabs. ... It is just not true that everything in this country is up for a vote. That would mean that if a bunch of white parents didn't want Black kids in their school anymore, they could vote on it."

What's Age Appropriate?

The other common complaint is that a material is not age appropriate. It's a compelling argument because any concerned parent or teacher is worried about children, especially young children, being exposed to inappropriate books, films, or class discussions. "One of the most

common ways that people, who in effect are calling for censorship, get around the stigma of that word is that they use the concept of age-appropriate," notes West. "It's a difficult criterion to nail down in real life with real children."

Issues of age appropriateness are most common in elementary and middle schools. Teachers, parents, and the courts have generally recognized that the older the student, the more that student has "the right to know." Of the questions about age-appropriate material, the one that schools seem least prepared to deal with, in part because it is relatively new, is the controversy over discussion of gay and lesbian families in the early elementary classroom.

One problem, says Frankfurt of GLSEN, is that "there's an assumption that if you talk about gay and lesbian people, the conversation will suddenly focus on homosexual sex. And that would be inappropriate in young grades. ... But when we talk about gay and lesbian issues to elementary students, we talk about families, we talk about love, we talk about relationships between two people — not sexual relationships, but the overall relationship."

In some districts, such as Provincetown, MA, conservatives have argued that the term gay and lesbian should not be used in class before the fourth or fifth grade. But such a prohibition prevents teachers taking a pro-active approach to dealing with issues of bias or being sensitive to the needs of children who may have gay parents. Further, it can even prevent teachers from taking more limited action. For example, it can tie a teacher's hands from responding to anti-gay name-calling. (Put-downs such as "faggot" or "that's so gay" are frequent playground taunts.)

"Such playground incidents are teachable moments," Frankfurt says. "Teach-

ers have a responsibility to let kids know that what they are saying is an insult. It is inappropriate and hurtful not only to people who are gay and lesbian but who may have gay and lesbian brothers, or aunts, or uncles."

Susan Hinkel, who helped found the now-disbanded Council on Interracial Books for Children, currently heads a non-profit group that works to help schools become more inclusive. When she is told that gay-themed books such as *Heather Has Two Mommies* or *Daddy's Roommate* are inappropriate for first graders she answers: "Are there gay families in your school? Are there children of gay families in your school? Children who have relatives who may be gay? If there are, then children are already asking all the questions that are answered thoughtfully in those books."

If teachers don't address questions that children may have about such issues, they are doing them a disservice, Hinkel argues. "When we hem and haw, or we don't give children a straight answer, we are silencing their questions, we are silencing their curiosity, we are silencing their permission to discuss."

Hinkel believes that the controversy over gay and lesbian themes is part of a broader pattern of silencing controversy in schools, in part because so many adults are uncomfortable talking about controversial issues. "We need to talk about censorship beyond the confines of print and video," she says, "and to talk about the dialogue and discussions that are censored in schools, about what is permissible to talk about and what is not permissible. ... We work in schools with children who are coming of age and yet the living issues that most affect them aren't talked about, in particular their identities. We don't talk about their race, their ethnicity, their sexual orientation, questions of 'who am I?' what is my spirituality, what is the difference between spirituality and religion, what is it to be male and female, how are we treating each other? It's not formal censorship, but it is almost absolute censorship."

Sadly, in most censorship cases, administrators or school board members rarely ask the students' opinions. Parental concerns are often paramount and students' opinions, let alone their rights, are usually an afterthought. As Quindlen said in a column on the *Where's Waldo* controversy, too often parents and administrators succumb "to an impulse that is at the heart of most book-banning in this country. And that is the temptation to treat kids like morons, to sell little people short."

The Controversial Huck Finn

Of all the books challenged in public schools, probably no other has received more publicity than *The Adventures of Huckleberry Finn* by Mark Twain. Controversy was particularly acute in the 1970s and 1980s, when books by non-white authors were far less common in the curriculum and *Huck Finn*, along with Harper Lee's *To Kill A Mockingbird,* were often the only high school literature books dealing with race. In recent years, *Huck*

book at heart is a stinging indictment of the racism of 19th century America. (For a look at how one African-American high school teacher decided to stop teaching *Huck Finn*, not because he was ordered to do so but because it just wasn't working with his students, see "Resisting the High School Canon," *Rethinking Schools,* Vol. 10, No. 4.) In most cases, schools have tried to reach a compromise that balances parental and community concerns, the need for academic freedom, and the educational and constitutional problems that arise when teachers are given mandates about what books they can or can't teach. When it comes to censorship, as with other issues of democracy, no strictly legal approach or administrative guideline can substitute for open lines of communication and a process of dialogue that allows everyone to be heard with respect and consideration.

Controversy over the book in the Kenosha, WI, school district provides an example of how the matter is often resolved. In 1995, the superintendent received a letter from John Wright, a representative of the NAACP, asking that *Huck Finn* be removed from the school curriculum because of its use of the term "nigger." Wright was asked to fill out the form,

clude the book from the curriculum. But it also argued that it would be inappropriate if "teachers uncomfortable with the tone of the book" were required to teach it.

"While it is the committee's desire to indicate support for the book, to do so at the expense of the teachers' freedom to choose appropriate materials is also detrimental," the committee decided.

The committee also recommended that when the book is used, it is within a context that explains the novel's historical background and explores issues of racism, language dialects, and the use of racial slurs. The committee also stressed that no student should be forced to read the book. Wright, meanwhile, dropped his threat of a lawsuit when the district agreed that a 1983 version of the book by the Chatham River Press, which was brought in by a teacher and was not a version acquired by the district, would not be used. Illustrations in the Chatham River edition were particularly offensive, with one of them showing a shiftless-looking Joe with a large piece of watermelon and the word "vittles" underneath.

Big Problems for Good Teachers

Joan Bertin of the National Coalition Against Censorship (NCAC) notes that historically, censorship has tended to be a tool of the status quo and of those in positions of authority. One of its main purposes has been to suppress dissent. Thus it is not surprising that many censorship cases involve issues such as the rights of gays and lesbians, as they move from the political margins and demand their inclusion as full members of society. Societal changes have also brought other issues into the forefront in recent years, such as teenage sexuality, divorce, drug use, and sexual abuse, and harassment. Finally, some cases of censorship appear to be part of the general backlash against multiculturalism, diversity, the opening up of school curricula to a broader array of perspectives than in the past.

Ironically, the teachers who get in trouble over censorship are often the teachers who are most sensitive to connecting their curriculum with their students' real lives and who don't flinch when students, either individually or as a class, want to

---

If controversial books and topics are avoided, how does that help students learn to critically evaluate differing opinions and make informed decisions?

Finn has been dropped from many required reading lists (as have other books from the traditional canon) and is usually offered only as an elective reading or as part of an elective course, according to West.

Complaints about *Huck Finn* have been raised by African-American parents and students who argue that the book's incessant use of the term "nigger" has a harmful effect on African-American students and contributes to racial animosity and stereotyping. Defenders of the book point out that, despite the surface language, the

"Citizen's Request for Reconsideration of a Book" and the matter was referred to a committee for review. "A high percentage of the committee included African-Americans due to the nature of the complaint," according to a summary of events from the district.

The committee looked at the book's literary merit, the "particular attitudes and words of its characters," and the "appropriateness of the book" in the curriculum, including the book's impact on African-American and white students. It found that there was insufficient cause to ex-

explore such topics. Adults may shun controversy but adolescents often thrive on it. As Suhor of the NCTE notes, "Teachers who plan well and teach excellently are often the very ones who are under attack in censorship cases."

What should teachers do, therefore, if a book they are using is challenged? Following are some of the guidelines developed by groups such as the NCTE, the AASA, and the ALA.

• Don't panic or act impulsively. Some teachers, administrators, and superintendents have a tendency to sidestep controversy by unilaterally pulling a book from the curriculum or school library. This only makes things worse.

• Always try and resolve the issue at the lowest level possible. If a parent is complaining, make sure their challenge is listened to and the parent is treated with respect. Many cases, if handled sensitively, need not get to the level of public acrimony and hearings before the school board.

• For curriculum materials, make sure you can explain the educational value of a book and how it fits into your curriculum.

• Help parents understand that part of learning to read better is acquiring the habit of reading for pleasure. Many children like scary stories, or goofy stories, or gross stories, even if they aren't Newberry award-winning books.

• Make sure your school and district have established policies in place to both select materials and handle challenges. Make sure the policies are followed consistently.

• If necessary, refer the controversy to a broadly based committee of teachers, educators, librarians, and parents.

• If it appears the issue will not be easily settled, don't wait to get outside help. This includes legal counsel, help with media relations, and support from national organizations involved in censorship cases. Teachers also need to be aware that what begins as a censorship issue can sometimes end up as a case of alleged "insubordination" (see article page 28).

The unfortunate reality is that a teacher or district can do all of the above and still end up on the front pages of the local newspaper for allegedly promoting smut, or homosexuality, or whatever the charge may be. When that happens, "it's admittedly going to be tough," notes Siegel of the ACLU. "But I would say to teachers that if they believe that the books or materials in question serve an important educational function in their curriculum, and if they can articulate that, then they probably have a constitutionally protected right to use that material."

As the saying goes, the Bill of Rights is only as strong as the paper it is written on — and the backbone of people willing to defend it. ■

Resources on Censorship

Following are some of the major organizations involved in censorship issues.

American Civil Liberties Union, 125 Broad St., 18th Floor, New York, NY 10004. 212-549-2500. E-mail: aclu@aclu.org. Internet: www.aclu.org. Probably the most vigilant group in the country when it comes to protecting legal rights to freedom of expression. Also provides information on a wide range of student rights. Be sure to check out its "Ask Sybil" series of popularly written handouts on student rights and its 181-page book, *The Rights of Students*.

The American Library Association Office for Intellectual Freedom, 50 E. Huron St., Chicago, IL 60611. 1-800-545-2433. Internet: www.ala.org. Provides a range of support and materials, including copies of reviews of controversial books and background on where the book has been challenged before. State and local library associations are also a good resource. Along with the American Association of School Administrators, the ALA published the 171-page book *Censorship and Selection: Issues and Answers for Schools*. One of the few books to deal with the specifics of censorship in schools, this is an invaluable resource. You can also get the book from the AASA, 1801 N. Moore St., Arlington, VA 22209. 703-528-0700.

National Coalition Against Censorship, 275 Seventh Ave., New York, NY 10001. 212-807-6222. E-mail: ncac@ncac.org. Internet: www.ncac.org. A coalition of almost 50 groups ranging from the American Federation of Teachers and the National Education Association to the Newspaper Guild, American Jewish Congress, International Reading Association, and the Writers Guild of America. Publishes a newsletter that keeps current with new cases of censorship.

National Council of Teachers of English, 1111 W. Kenyon Road, Urbana, IL 61801. 800-369-6283; 217-328-3870. Internet: www.ncte.org. Has a standing committee dealing with censorship in schools and provides a variety of materials. Because it is a teacher-based organization, the NCTE is particularly sensitive to how censorship issues play out in schools.

People for the American Way, 2000 M St., NW, Suite 400, Washington, DC 20036. 202-467-4999. E-mail: pfaw@pfaw.org. Internet: www.pfaw.org. PFAW has a particularly good feel for the politics of censorship and how censorship is used by the religious right as part of a broader attack on public education. Also covers issues such as vouchers, creationism, sexuality education, and "parental rights" initiatives.

This article first appeared in *Rethinking Schools*, Spring 1998 (Vol. 12, No. 3).

Frequently Challenged Books

Following are some of the most frequently challenged books and the objections raised. The challenges range from demands that the book be removed from the curriculum, either as mandatory or elective reading, to demands that it be pulled from the school library. Because of the local nature of book challenges, it is difficult to list the books in any definitive order. The list is based on information from People for the American Way and the American Library Association.

• *I Know Why the Caged Bird Sings*, by Maya Angelou. Description of a rape; complaints the book is "anti-white."

• *The Giver*, by Lois Lowry. Condones infanticide, endorses abortion, and promotes new age practices such as guided imagery.

• *The Adventures of Huckleberry Finn*, by Mark Twain. Incessant use of the word "nigger."

• *Of Mice and Men*, by John Steinbeck. Profanity.

• *The Color Purple*, by Alice Walker. Too violent and sexually graphic and deals with lesbianism.

• *The Chocolate War*, by Robert Cormier. Profane language and sexual content.

• *Go Ask Alice*, Anonymous (diary of a teenage drug user). Depictions of drug use, sexual situations, and suicide.

• *The Catcher in the Rye*, by J. D. Salinger. Uses the "f" word and portrays prostitution, teenage depression, and alienation.

• *A Day No Pigs Would Die*, by Robert Newton Peck. "Gory" descriptions of two pigs mating, a pig being slaughtered, and a cow giving birth.

• *Native Son*, by Richard Wright. Sexually graphic and violent; uses the word "nigger."

• *My Brother Sam is Dead*, by Christopher and James Lincoln Collier. Profanity and graphic depictions of war.

• *Bridge to Terabithia*, by Katherine Paterson. Profanity, disrespect of adults, and an elaborate fantasy world that "might

lead to confusion."

• *Goosebumps Series*, by R. L. Stine. Violence and glorification of the occult.

• *It's Perfectly Normal*, by Robie Harris (a sex education book). Discussions of sexuality, including homosexuality.

• *Forever*, by Judy Blume. Sexual themes.

• *Scary Stories to Tell in the Dark*, by Alvin Schwartz. Overly violent and frightening and "dabbles in the occult."

• *More Scary Stories to Tell in the Dark*, by Alvin Schwartz.

• *Scary Stories 3: More Tales to Chill Your Bones*, by Alvin Schwartz.

• *Halloween ABC*, by Even Merriam. Halloween is of pagan origin and the book is "evil." ∎

The National Council of Teachers of English (NCTE) has developed a series of responses to many of the books listed, in which classroom teachers have outlined their educational rationale for keeping the book in either the curriculum or library. The NCTE is in the process of compiling the responses on a CD-Rom, which should be available in coming months. For information contact the NCTE, 1-800-369-6283.

Know the Law

In 1965, a group of middle school students in Des Moines decided to wear black armbands to school to protest the Vietnam War. District principals learned of the plan and prohibited the wearing of armbands, arguing they wanted to prevent possible disturbances. Several students defied the ban, wore armbands, and were suspended.

The case, *Tinker v. Des Moines Independent School District,* ended up before the U.S. Supreme Court. In what is one of the most-often quoted affirmations of free speech in schools, the 7-2 majority wrote in its 1969 decision, "It can hardly be argued that either students or teachers shed their constitutional rights to freedom of speech or expression at the schoolhouse gate."

Tinker is one of four key U.S. Supreme Court cases outlining the legal parameters of issues of school censorship. The second major case is *Board of Education, Island Trees (New York) Union Free School District 26 v. Pico.*

The Pico Case

In September 1975, three members of the school board of the Island Trees school district on Long Island attended a conference of the conservative group, Parents of New York United. There they received a list of "objectionable" books, ranging from *Soul On Ice* by Eldridge Cleaver to *The Fixer* by Bernard Malamud and *The Best Short Stories by Negro Writers,* edited by Langston Hughes. The board members discovered that nine of the listed books were in their high school library and another was in the junior high library. They directed that the books be removed, justifying their action on the grounds that the books were "anti-American, anti-Christian, anti-[Semitic], and just plain filthy."

In June 1982, the U.S. Supreme Court ruled 5-4 that school officials "may not remove books from school library shelves simply because they dislike the ideas contained in those books. ..."

Justice William J. Brennan, in the lead opinion, argued that "Just as access to

ideas makes it possible for citizens generally to exercise their rights of free speech and press in a meaningful manner, such access prepares students for active and effective participation in the pluralistic, often contentious society in which they will soon be adult members."

But even Brennan conceded that school boards "have significant discretion to determine the content of their school libraries." That phrase, and the opinions of the court minority (which included current U.S. Supreme Court Chief Justice William Rehnquist), are important cautions. Whether one agrees or not, the Supreme Court has recognized that censorship issues in the schools abide by different rules than censorship cases in public libraries, bookstores, and other non-school settings.

The heart of the complexities involve the conflicting views of the role of public schools in society. As the book *Censorship and Selection* notes: "If a school's role is seen primarily as one of indoctrination and inculcation of community values, school boards will have almost unlimited discretion in the selection and removal of materials that are part of the school's curriculum. If, however, the view is that the school is a marketplace of ideas where students may have access to a variety of viewpoints, the limits imposed upon the school board are expanded considerably. Both these views are held to varying degrees by judges at all levels, including the United States Supreme Court."

Pico narrowly tilted toward the side of the marketplace of ideas. Two subsequent decisions tilted toward school officials' right to select, limit, and indoctrinate.

The Fraser Case

The third case, *Bethel School District v. Fraser,* involved 14-year-old Matthew Fraser's campaign speech for a friend during a voluntary school assembly at Bethel High School in Pierce County, WA. The speech was laced with sexual metaphor and innuendo but no actual sexual terms. For example, Fraser talked about how his friend was "a man who is firm."

In 1986 the Supreme Court upheld the suspension 7-2. The court distinguished between the political "message" in *Tinker* and the sexual content of Fraser's speech. It argued that it is appropriate for schools to prohibit the use of vulgar and offensive terms, and that a school "need not tolerate student speech that is inconsistent with its 'basic educational mission.'"

The Hazelwood Decision

The fourth case — *Hazelwood School District v. Kuhlmeier* — began in 1983 when students at Hazelwood East High School in St. Louis County, MO published two controversial articles in the school newspaper. One described an unnamed student's experiences with pregnancy and the other discussed the impact of divorce on students at the school. The principal ordered the stories removed. One of his arguments was that the pregnancy article's references to sexual activity and birth control were "inappropriate" for younger students at the school.

In what is considered a setback to the right of students to self-expression, the U.S. Supreme Court ruled in 1988 that school officials may censor stories in official school publications as long as "their actions are reasonably related to legitimate pedagogical concerns." The ruling, however, rested on a principal's authority over school curriculum, such as official publications, school plays or other school-sponsored activity. Underground newspapers produced without a teacher's help, or other free speech issues such as a student's right to wear political buttons, remain subject only to the *Tinker* standard.

While *Hazelwood* tempers previous Supreme Court decisions, it does not overrule them. School officials must show a "legitimate pedagogical purpose" when they make decisions on banning or selecting materials. As the ACLU notes in its book, *The Rights of Students,* nothing in the *Hazelwood* decision "gives a principal the right to censor an article because of disagreement with its point of view." ∎

Is Teaching 'La Causa' Grounds for Firing?

Patsy and Nadine Cordova were considered outstanding teachers in the small town of Vaughn, N.M. But in June 1996 they helped students at Vaughn Junior and Senior High School organize a MEChA club, a common student group in the Southwest which stands for Movimiento Estudiantil Chicano de Aztlan. And that, they believe, is when their troubles began.

That fall, Vaughn Superintendent Arthur Martinez told the Cordova sisters they could not teach anything "that reflects the MEChA philosophy." He accused Nadine of teaching "racial intolerance" and promoting "a militant attitude" in her students.

Under legal advice, the Cordova sisters asked that any further curriculum directives from Martinez be in writing. They believed that the superintendent's directives not only violated their rights under the First Amendment but were counter to the district's policies on handling complaints about curriculum. Nonetheless, they sought to comply until their lawyers could resolve matters.

By January of 1997, relations between

union.

But the prohibitions went beyond the UFW. The sisters were also told "to eliminate any reference to or discussion of Robert Kennedy, the U.S. Constitution, Dolores Huerta, justice, courage or non-violence," according to Nadine's attorney, Richard Rosenstock of the New Mexico Civil Liberties Union.

The controversy escalated when the Albuquerque newspaper ran a front-page story on Feb. 15 titled, "Chicano Studies Out in Vaughn." Rosenstock told *Rethinking Schools* that Martinez and his allies on the board were furious about the article. "As soon as this article comes out, he [Martinez] starts soliciting complaints from people from six or eight years ago and starts to put together a case against the

Nadine Cordova.

At a board meeting Feb. 26 allegedly set up to resolve the problems, Martinez asked the sisters if they would stop using the Teaching Tolerance materials. The sisters said they would do so only if the request were in writing.

The Cordova sisters got an answer, of sorts, two days later. The town's chief of police walked into the school and handed them a letter telling them they were suspended on grounds of insubordination. That July, the board fired them. (For an excellent article on the case, see the August/September 1997 issue of *Teacher.*)

The Cordova sisters have filed suit in federal court to get their jobs back. They are confident they will win.

"I think somewhere along the line they thought they were going to scare us off, and that was going to be it," Patsy told *Teacher* magazine. "And now they have to prove it. And they can't." ■

> ### *The Cordova sisters were told to eliminate any reference to the UFW, "la causa," or even the U.S. Constitution.*

---

the sisters and the superintendent were strained. Martinez told the sisters in writing that they could not use the supplementary text *500 Years of Chicano History*, could not study Cesar Chavez and the UFW, or hand out any materials that promote "la causa." Nadine argues that agricultural interests in the area were particularly concerned that students learning about Chavez and the United Farm Workers

Cordova sisters."

On Feb. 21, 1997, the sisters informed Martinez in writing that they hoped to use materials from the group Teaching Tolerance. They enclosed the table of contents from the group's curriculum package *The Shadow of Hate: A History of Intolerance in America,* a copy of some articles, and the kit's statement of purpose. Martinez did not respond.

Internet Filtering: Beware the Cybercensors

by Barbara Miner

I magine if an unknown person came into your school library every month and removed books from the shelves. You would never be told which books were being taken or why, other than that someone, somewhere, deemed them "inappropriate," "indecent," "radical," "tasteless," or "gross." Imagine if the books included works on the Holocaust, Islam, AIDS/HIV, gay rights, the National Organization for Women, or the International Workers of the World union.

Couldn't ever happen? Guess again.

Under the guise of protecting children from "smut" and "indecency," Internet filtering programs routinely block access to thousands of World Wide Web pages, chat-rooms, newsgroups and other Internet options — including the topics listed above. What's more, if Sen. John McCain (R-Ariz.) gets his way, Congress will pass legislation mandating that school districts must use filtering software if they want to receive discounts on telecommunications services, or what is known as the E-rate.

Groups fighting censorship, in particular organizations which want to nurture the democratic potential of the Internet, are hoping to scuttle the legislation. They also want to alert the public to the dark underside of seemingly innocuous filtering programs.

"The word 'filter' is much too kind to these programs. It conjures up inaccurate, gee-whiz images of sophisticated, discerning choice," Seth Finkelstein, a founder of The Censorware Project, said in testimony on the McCain bill this spring. "When these products are examined in detail, they usually turn out to be the crudest of blacklists, long tables of hapless material which has run afoul of a stupid computer program or person, perhaps offended by the word 'breast' (as in possibly 'breast cancer') ... ."

Under the guise of protecting children from "indecency," filters routinely block thousands of web pages, chat rooms, and newsgroups dealing with feminist, gay, and "radical" issues.

Such warnings are more than political rhetoric. Every filtering program that has been examined in detail, for instance, has placed feminist organizations on its list of censored sites, according to The Censorware Project, an on-line group founded by computer software experts, free speech advocates, and Internet activists. A number of filtering software companies have even blocked sites reporting on political and technical problems with the software.

Filtering programs are "a bait-and-switch maneuver," argue Brock Meeks and Declan McCullagh, authors of a 1996 filtering exposé in the e-mail publication *CyberWire Dispatch*. "The smut-censors say they're going after porn, but they quietly restrict political speech."

Michael Sims of The Censorware Project cautions that people need to be skeptical of claims by filtering companies that they are technically capable of thoughtfully reviewing the million of pages on the World Wide Web. "Everyone knows that a standard automobile doesn't get 200 miles per gallon of gas, so that claim is unrealistic," Sims told *Rethinking Schools*. "But people don't understand that some of the claims of censorware makers are equally unrealistic."

Communications Decency Act

Protecting children from pornography on the Internet is clearly an important issue. The discussion, however, has been dominated by fear, scare stories, and political posturing. Opponents of censorship are especially worried that some groups, especially politicians and organizations affiliated with the religious right, are using legitimate concerns about protecting children to push through a broader agenda of "cleaning up" the free-wheeling world of the Internet and imposing a moralistically and politically narrow view of the world.

One of the most important Internet censorship battles involved the Communications Decency Act (CDA). Passed by Congress in the fall of 1996, the bill would, in practice, have banned "indecency" from the Internet as a way of protecting children from "patently offensive" material. Those sections of the law involving the Internet were found unconstitutional by the U.S. Supreme Court in June of 1997. The CDA was "a creature of the religious right, which had a significant hand in sculpting it, lining up politicians to support it, and then supplying them with the ammunition they needed to get it passed," according to Jonathan Wallace, author of the book *Sex, Laws, and Cyberspace* and a founder of the Internet magazine *The Ethical Spectacle*.

The U.S. Supreme Court's decision on the CDA has been called "the first free speech ruling of the 21st Century." In it, the court argues that the Internet is akin to printed material, not to radio or television, and deserves the highest free speech protections. It reiterates that the Internet

"is a unique and wholly new medium of worldwide human communication," and that it is "no exaggeration to conclude that the content on the Internet is as diverse as human thought." (The beginning pages of the majority decision are a wonderful summary of the Internet's origins, scope and potential. The ruling can be downloaded from: http://supct.law.cornell.edu/supct/html/96-511.ZO.html.

Both sides in the CDA suit stipulated as fact that, while pornography is available on the web, almost all sexually explicit images are preceded by warnings. The "odds are slim" that users would encounter such material accidentally, according to the court.

Having been set back in the courts, religious right groups and their allies turned toward imposing filtering software in public libraries and schools. In a typical story, the conservative *Washington Times* wrote a story in October 1997 with the headline: "Cyberporn at libraries has smut

foes furious: We need to keep pornography out of taxpayer facilities." A story that December in the *Weekly Standard* was titled: "Quiet in the Library! Children Viewing Porn." The magazine, generally considered the leading conservative newsweekly, criticized the American Library Association for its concern with censorship and the use of filtering software in public libraries. It then asked:

So, what should conservatives do in response? They could adopt a libertarian stance: shut down the libraries and let citizens do their own Web searches at home, with or without filters. Or they could try to take the libraries back from the American Library Association; perhaps local politicians could fire recalcitrant librarians, which would free up cash for computer-equipped charter schools whose librarians treat parents' concerns with respect. The Republican Congress could pass a law that helps parents sue librarians who fail to take reasonable measures [against indecency] ... Congress

could even go a step further and prod the Justice Department to jail careless librarians when the computers under their charge are used to break the law.

Charged Atmosphere

It's not surprising that many school districts have decided to use filtering software. Given legitimate concerns about protecting children from pornography and age-inappropriate material, coupled with the highly charged political atmosphere that surrounds all school issues, they may feel that they have little choice. "Obviously, schools need to be concerned about some of the materials that people are producing that may not be appropriate for kids," notes Gary Marx of the American Association of School Administrators. "If schools don't worry about it, then they will be told very quickly by people in the community, if there is an incident, that they had better be concerned."

As more information becomes available about filtering software, a growing number of media, education, and computer groups are advising caution. For instance, the Journalism Education Association, which represents middle and high school journalism teachers and advisors for school papers, passed a resolution in November that "strongly opposes the use of filters or blocking software." Other groups concerned about filtering software range from the American Society of Newspaper Editors to Computer Professionals for Social Responsibility, Feminists for Free Expression, the PEN American Center, and the Society of Professional Journalists.

The controversy centers around the use of filtering software by governmental bodies such as public libraries or school districts. The fear is that in using the software, the libraries and school put themselves in the position of allowing the filter to act as a censor.

Critics of filtering software make two main points. First, school districts and public libraries need to be aware of how filtering works — that it blocks out any number of legitimate sites and, conversely, often fails to block "indecent" sites. Second, particularly for schools, using filters may be at the expense of the more educationally sound practice of teaching kids how to responsibly use and evaluate the Internet. (This article focuses on filtering software; an equally important issue for school districts is developing Appropriate Use Policies that govern a range of Internet issues, from student use of e-mail, to recreational versus educational use of the Internet at school, to disciplinary actions when Internet policies are violated. One of the most important issues is teaching children safety issues on the Internet — for example that they should never give out their name, phone number, or address to strangers on the net.)

Most Popular Filters

Some of the major filtering software products are CYBERsitter, Cyber Patrol, Net Nanny, BESS, X-Stop, SmartFilter and SafeSurf. The software is produced by private companies which, in order to protect and sell their product, don't want to be too specific about how the software works or release a list of what sites are blocked.

The sheer immensity of the web — a recent study estimates there are roughly 320 million separate web pages — makes human evaluation of all web pages mathematically impossible.

But just suppose a librarian or school official did get a copy of the blacklist. They probably wouldn't have time to evaluate it thoroughly. Cyber Patrol claims to have over 50,000 blocked entries, and each entry can ban as little as one web page or as much as an entire domain. At a minute per entry, that's more than 100 workdays just to give a cursory inspection, according to Finkelstein of The Censorware Project. A few minutes of math calculations "should immediately destroy the myth that a librarian or schoolteacher can look over a product and make more than insignificant adjustments for his or her own values," Finkelstein argues.

As a result, schools and libraries have to take on faith that the filtering company is doing a good job. That faith may be misplaced, however.

A growing number of organizations are investigating and exposing how filtering software works. One such group is the cyber-organization Peacefire: Youth Alliance Against Internet Censorship. The group was founded in August 1996 to represent students' and minors' interests in the debate over freedom of speech on the Internet. Full membership is limited to people under 21. On its web site, Peacefire notes: "There were very few people in mid-1996 speaking out against blocking software programs like CYBERsitter and Cyber Patrol, because most adults would not be affected by the proliferation of these programs." (Anyone interested in not only filtering software but the power of youth organizing should check out Peacefire's site: www.peacefire.org.)

Peacefire maintains a list of some of the sites blocked by various filters. One of the more far-reaching filtering programs appears to be CYBERsitter, which has been marketed in part by the religious right organization Focus on the Family. In its options for filtering, CYBERsitter includes the categories, "advocating illegal/radical activities" and "gay/lesbian activities."

Some of the sites that have been blocked by CYBERsitter include:
• The National Organization for Women.
• The International Gay and Lesbian Human Rights Commission.
• Yahoo web search for "gay rights."
• The Peacefire web site.

CYBERsitter apparently was upset with Peacefire because of its exposé of blocked sites. CYBERsitter even went to Peacefire's Internet provider, Media3, and threatened to block the pages of all the other domain names on the Media3 server if Peacefire were not removed from the server, according to an article in the Dec. 6, 1996, *WIRED News*. Media3 threatened legal action if CYBERsitter followed through on its threats.

One of the first articles to blow the whistle on filtering programs was the *CyberWire Dispatch* article "Keys to the Kingdom" (available at www.eff.org/pub/Publications; look for Declan McCullagh collection). "CYBERSitter doesn't hide the fact that they're trying to enforce a moral code," according to the article. When CYBERsitter CEO Brian Milburn was asked about the National Organization for Women's (NOW) concern that its site was blocked, he responded, "If NOW doesn't like it, tough ... We have not and will not bow to any pressure from any organization that disagrees with our philosophy."

Other software filtering companies may be less overtly political but they nonetheless have blocked a range of worthwhile pages. Take Cyber Patrol. According to Peacefire, sites and newsgroups that have been blocked by Cyber Patrol include:
• The MIT Student Association for Freedom of Expression.

• Planned Parenthood.

• Nizkor, a Holocaust remembrance page.

• Envirolink, a clearinghouse of environmental information on the Internet.

• Mother Jones magazine online.

• The soc.feminism newsgroup.

• The AOL Sucks web site ("Why American On Line Sucks.")

(If you want to check out these filtering programs, go to their websites. For CYBERsitter it's www.solidoak.com; for CyberPatrol it's www.cyberpatrol.com. The Cyber Patrol logo is telling. It consists of a police-type badge and the slogan: "To Surf and Protect.")

CyberWire Dispatch calls Cyber Patrol "easily the largest and most extensive smut-blocker. It assigns each undesirable web site to at least one and often multiple categories that range from 'violence/profanity' to 'sexual acts,' 'drugs and drug culture,' and 'gross depictions.'" What, one might ask, constitutes "gross depictions?" One answer is, animal rights pages — such as a blocked page which shows syphilis-infected monkeys.

Wallace, of *The Ethical Spectacle,* points out the tendency of filters to block based on political content. His magazine — which he describes as "a sober, intellectual, rather dry publication, without prurient photographs or stories, which aspires to be an electronic equivalent of print magazines like *The Nation, The National Review,* or *The Atlantic* — has been blocked by seven censorware products. "And those are only the ones I know about," he says.

Finkelstein of The Censorware Project notes that CyberPatrol blocked his site on Internet Labeling and Rating Systems (part of the MIT Student Association for Freedom of Expression, www.mit.edu/activities/safe), under categories ranging from Full Nudity to Militant/Extreme to Satanic/Cult.

Blocking worthwhile pages is only part of the problem. If the goal is protecting children from pornography, many of the filtering softwares don't block what should be blocked. An article in the Focus on the Family magazine noted that *Consumer Reports* tested four of the biggest Internet filters. "The results were discouraging,"

Filtering software companies make it seem that decisions are being carefully made by reasonable people whose only goal is protecting children. But in reality, filtering software generally relies on scanning a site's keywords or its URL, rather than actually looking at a site.

according to Focus on the Family. "After selecting 22 'easy-to-find' objectionable Web sites, technical experts attempted to log onto those sites with the blocking software running. SurfWatch tested the best, with only four sites getting past the software. Cyber Patrol let six sites slip through, CYBERsitter missed eight, and Net Nanny let all 22 through."

The Focus on the Family article also complained that filtering software had blocked "Christian videos that deal with sexuality."

Who Holds the Power?

One of the unanswered questions about filtering software is: who decides and how? Filtering software companies make it seem that decisions are being carefully made by reasonable people whose only goal is protecting children. But in reality, filtering software generally relies on scanning a site's keywords or its URL, rather than actually looking at a site. That is why, for example, if a filtering software is looking to block anything with the word "sex," it will potentially eliminate sites about Middlesex, England or the poetry of Anne Sexton.

The article "Keys to the Kingdom" notes that Cyber Patrol doesn't even store the complete URL for blocking and instead abbreviates the last three characters. Thus, for instance, Shawn Knight had an occult resources page, located at Carnegie Mellon University, and the final coding for his site began with the letters "sha." Cyber Patrol blocked 23 other accounts at Carnegie Mellon University with "sha" as the first three letters of the final coding — including Derrick "Shadow" Brasherr's web page on Pittsburgh radio stations. When the filter blocked the

"CyberOS" gay video available through the Internet Service Provider webcom.com, it also blocked 17 other sites at the server that started with "cyb" — including a site billed as the first "Cyber High School."

The sheer immensity of the web — a recent study in the journal *Science* estimates there are roughly 320 million separate web pages — makes human evaluation of web pages impossible, according to Internet experts. Sims of The Censorware Project notes that Digital Equipment Corporation's search engine AltaVista — perhaps the fastest search engine, with a bandwidth so powerful it could support 87 million phone lines — adds a new page in a fraction of a second and still only has about 28% of the web in its database. "No censorware company has more than a tiny fraction of AltaVista's bandwidth," Sims notes. "No censorware company has more than fraction of the hardware, or technical expertise, of the people at Digital Equipment Corporation. And supposedly these pages are viewed by a human, taking a minute or more instead of a split second?"

It is "mathematically impossible to 'view' any significant portion of the web," according to Sims.

Family-Friendly Search Engines

Ever on the prowl for a new product or gimmick to sell to parents and schools, computer software companies are developing "family friendly search engines." If filtering can be compared to taking books out of the library and storing them in an inaccessible back room, "family friendly search engines" are akin to taking a student to the Library of Congress but not letting them use the card catalog.

What is being billed as "the world's first family friendly Internet search site" was released this past October by Net Shepherd and AltaVista and called Net Shepherd Family Search. According to Net Shepherd's web site, the search engine filters out web sites "judged by an independent panel of demographically appropriate Internet users, to be inappropriate and/or objectionable to the average user families."

The Electronic Privacy Information Center (EPIC), a Washington-D.C-based public interest research center established in 1994, has released a study on Net Shepherd's Family Search engine. In the study, it conducted 100 searches using AltaVista, a traditional search engine, and Net Shepherd's Family Search. Requests ranged from phrases such as "American Red Cross," to the "San Diego Zoo," to the "Smithsonian Institution," to potentially controversial topics such as the "Bill of Rights," "Christianity" and "eating disorders."

"In every case in our sample, we found that the family-friendly search engine prevented us from obtaining access to almost 90% of the materials on the Internet containing the relevant search terms," according to EPIC. "We further found that in many cases, the search service denied access to 99% of the material that would otherwise be available without the filters." For example:

• The non-filtered search for "NAACP" listed 4,000 documents. The Family search produced 15 documents.

• The non-filtered search for "Thomas Edison" came up with 11,552 documents. On Family Search: nine.

And poor Dr. Seuss. Only eight of the 2,653 references on AltaVista relating to Dr. Seuss were available through Family Search — and one of them was a parody of a Dr. Seuss story using details from the murder of Nicole Brown Simpson.

"While it is true that there is material available on the Internet that some will find legitimately objectionable, it is also clear that in some cases the proposed solutions may be worse than the actual problem," EPIC noted. The most important task is for parents and teachers to take an active role in guiding children's use of the Internet. As EPIC notes: "Helping children tell right from wrong is not something that should be left to computer software or search engines." ■

Barbara Miner is managing editor of *Rethinking Schools*. This article first appeared in *Rethinking Schools*, Summer 1998 (Vol. 12, No. 4).

Resources on Internet Censorship

Not surprisingly, the best resources are available on-line. There are any number of good sites to get you started and most have links to other sites. While these resources focus on issues of censorship and filtering software, there will also be links to other Internet issues of interest to schools, such as teaching children about safety issues on the net, or appropriate use policies.

Two good sites to start out are the web pages of the American Civil Liberties Union and People for the American Way Foundation; both deal not only with censorship on the Internet but censorship and civil liberties issues in general.

American Civil Liberties Union. www.aclu.org. Be sure to check out its Cyber-Liberties pages on the site. The ACLU has also published a valuable report, *Fahrenheit 451.2: Is Cyberspace Burning?* The report is a comprehensive look at another proposal with worrisome implications for censorship — a ratings system of web pages.

People for the American Way Foundation. www.pfaw.org. Like the ACLU, PFAW has played a leading role in legal challenges to censorship on the net. Check out its pages on Free Expression, in particular, information on its lawsuit against filtering software in the public library in Loudon, VA.

Computer Professionals for Social Responsibility. Has an especially good page on Frequently Asked Questions about filters. www.cpsr.org.

Electronic Frontier Foundation. www.eff.org. This non-profit group working to protect privacy, free expression, and democracy online has an extensive site with extensive links. Ironically, its censorship archive was blocked by CyberPatrol.

Electronic Privacy Information Center. www.epic.org. A public interest research center in Washington, D.C. established in 1994, EPIC is a project of the Fund for Constitutional Government. Its report on family friendly search engines is at: www.epic.org.

The Ethical Spectacle. www.spectacle.org. An on-line magazine founded by Jonathan Wallace, co-author of *Sex, Laws, and Cyberspace* — of which *The New York Times* said, "required reading for anyone interested in free speech in modern society." (New York, Henry Holt & Co: 1997). The site also hosts The Censorware Project.

Internet Free Express Alliance. www.ifea.net. Resources page is especially good. Members include ACLU, American Society of Newspaper Editors, Feminists for Free Expression, National Coalition Against Censorship, National Association of Artists Organizations, and the Society of Professional Journalists.

The MIT Student Association for Freedom of Expression (SAFE) Home Page. www.mit.edu/activities/safe. This page has lots of good information and links on filtering software. One stop here and you'll easily be on your way to any number of other good sites.

Peacefire: Youth Alliance Against Internet Censorship. www.peacefire.org. A dynamite site for anyone interested in filtering software and/or youth organizing.

U.S. Supreme Court majority opinion on the Communications Decency Act. http://supct.law.cornell.edu/supct/ or http://www2.epic.org/cda/cda_decision.html#majority.

Jean-Claude Lejeune

CREATIONISM

Wrapped in a Cloak of Pseudo-science

The Evolution of Creationism

by Leon Lynn

More than 70 years after the Scopes "Monkey Trial," the scientific theory of evolution is still too hot for some American schools to handle.

In that infamous 1925 case, worldwide attention focused on John T. Scopes, who was on trial for teaching evolution and breaking a Tennessee law which banned teaching "any theory that denies the story of the Divine Creation of man as taught in the Bible." Despite decades of scientific advances supporting evolution since the Scopes trial, despite numerous court rulings aimed at protecting science and educators from religious zealotry, and despite ever-increasing rhetoric about helping students compete in the modern world by giving them the best possible science education, schools all across the country are under pressure to downplay, ignore, or distort one of the fundamental theories of modern science. In at least some of those schools, the pressure is working.

What's more, some observers say, the pressure is getting worse. Right-wingers and religious fundamentalists have been buoyed by newfound political strength in recent years. They are attacking evolution — as well as the whole concept of a secular, publicly funded school system — with ever-increasing vigor as they attempt to batter down the U.S. Constitution's separation of church and state and stamp their own brand of religion upon school curriculum. Creationists don't often win outright victories; a court decision or legislative vote eventually stops many anti-evolution proposals. Nonetheless, the enemies of evolution often succeed in sending a message to teachers: If you value your careers, don't teach this. And many teachers, fearing they'll be fired or that their communities will shun them, comply.

Furthermore, in recent years creationists have adopted more sophisticated tactics. In particular, they have repackaged creationism to make such beliefs appear as legitimate scientific theory — and which they then argue should be taught in conjunction with evolution.

Will teachers be intimidated by creationism and evade the teaching of evolution?

Jean-Claude Lejeune

What is Evolution?

Simply put, evolution is the scientific theory that all life forms on earth today are descended from a single cell, or at most a very few different cells. The diversity we see among species is the result of biological changes that have taken place over many hundreds of millions of years. During that time, new variations of plants and animals have appeared, through what the National Association of Biology Teachers terms "an unsupervised, impersonal, unpredictable, and natural process of tem-

poral descent ... ." Those new variations best able to adapt — to find food, escape predators, protect living space, or produce offspring — survived to pass along their traits to future generations. This is the process that Charles Darwin termed "natural selection" in his seminal 1859 work, *On the Origin of Species by Means of Natural Selection*.

The scientific community attaches great importance to the theory of evolution. The National Association of Biology Teachers says it's impossible to provide "a rational, coherent and scientific account" of the history and diversity of organisms on earth, or to effectively teach cellular and molecular biology, without including the principles and mechanisms of evolution. Similarly, leading national voices for the reform of science education, including the National Science Teachers Association and the American Association for the Advancement of Science, emphasize the importance of teaching evolution as part of a well-rounded K-12 science curriculum. An NSTA position paper on evolution, for example, notes that there is "abundant and consistent evidence from astronomy, physics, biochemistry, geochronology, geology, biology, anthropology, and other sciences that evolution has taken place," making it an important "unifying concept for science." Scientific disciplines "with a historical component, such as astronomy, geology, biology, and anthropology, cannot be taught with integrity if evolution is not emphasized," NSTA concludes.

What Creationists Believe

Generally, there's no conflict today between the theory of evolution and the religious beliefs of people who think that a supernatural entity guided the creation of the world. Many scientists and philosophers who accept the validity of evolution are nevertheless devoutly religious. Even Pope John Paul II, in a statement released in 1996, said that while the Catholic church holds that God created heaven and Earth, there is strong scientific evidence to support evolution.

In the realm of U.S. politics and education, however, the term creationist is generally used to refer to people actively pushing a particular, fundamentalist Christian religious perspective which rejects the theory of evolution as false. While there are different factions — some creationists insist that Earth is only a few thousand years old, for example, while others remain open to the possibility that it's much older — people actively challenging evolution and seeking to promote creationism generally believe that:

• Life appeared on Earth suddenly, in forms similar or identical to those seen today. Humans, therefore, did not evolve from earlier species.

• All life was designed for certain functions and purposes.

• The Bible is an accurate historical record of creation and other events, such as the Great Flood. (Again, however, there

Right-wing fundamentalists are attacking evolution with ever-increasing vigor as they attempt to batter down the U.S. Constitution's separation of church and state and stamp their brand of religion upon school curriculum.

are factional differences. Some creationists insist that the "creation week" was a literal seven-day week, while others believe the creation period could have lasted longer.)

Many creationists also believe that because evolution contradicts their interpretation of the Bible, it is therefore anti-God. For example Henry Morris, founder of a leading creationist think tank, the Institute for Creation Research, has written that evolution is dangerous because it leads "to the notion that each person owns himself, and is the master of his own destiny." This, he argues, is "contrary to the Bible teaching that man is in rebellion against God." (See the "Resources" on page 46 for more information on the Institute for Creation Research.)

The Roots of Creationism

In the decades immediately following the publication of Darwin's landmark book in 1859, colleges began revising their curricula "to purge religious influences," says Gerald R. Skoog, a professor of education at Texas Tech University and a past president of the National Science Teachers Association. High schools began following suit around 1900, but the process was by no means swift or comprehensive. In 1925 in Dayton, TN, science teacher John T. Scopes was put on trial for breaking a Tennessee state law which banned the teaching of evolution. The case became an international spectacle because of the appearances, and impassioned arguments, of lawyer Clarence Darrow on Scopes' behalf and political giant William Jennings Bryan in opposition to evolution. Scopes was convicted, although his conviction was later dismissed on appeal by the state Supreme Court. The anti-evolution law remained

on the books in Tennessee until 1967, when it was finally repealed.

In recent decades, numerous state and federal court decisions have sought to protect scientists and educators who advocate the teaching of evolution. At the heart of the decisions is the courts' view that banning the teaching of evolution is a violation of the U.S. Constitution's separation of church and state. Among the more significant decisions:

• The U.S. Supreme Court ruled in 1968 that an Arkansas law banning the teaching of evolution was unconstitutional. In essence, the court held that creationists were attempting to foist a particular religious philosophy in the schools.

• In 1981 the Supreme Court rejected a California creationist's claim that classroom discussions of evolution infringed on his right, and the rights of his children, to free exercise of religion.

• In 1987, the Supreme Court tossed out a Louisiana law that required the teaching of creationism whenever evolution was taught in schools, saying the law was an endorsement of religion.

• In 1990, the Seventh Circuit Court of Appeals ruled that a school district could prohibit a teacher from teaching creationism and that such a prohibition wouldn't violate the teacher's free-speech rights.

• Similarly, in 1994 the Ninth Circuit Court of Appeals ruled that a teacher's First Amendment right to free exercise of religion is not violated by a school-district requirement that teachers include evolution in biology curricula.

• In September 1997, a U.S. district court in Louisiana struck down as unconstitutional a three-year-old policy in Tangipahoa Parish that required teachers to read a disclaimer before teaching the theory of evolution.

Evolution also received a major boost, oddly enough, from the Soviet Union's launch of Sputnik in 1957. Critics of the U.S. education system seized on the launch, saying America's "defeat" in the space race was due to poor schooling. This issue quickly became part of the national political agenda, and schools began putting new emphasis on math and science education.

Despite these court decisions, however, and the resurgence of interest in science education that flowed from the space race, evolution remains a popular target in school board meeting rooms, legislative halls, and courthouses from Virginia to California. The last decade in particular has seen a surge in creationist political activity.

On the Rise

"It certainly looks as though it's on the rise," says Eugenie Scott, executive director of the National Center for Science Education, which advocates the teaching of evolution and opposes allowing creationism in schools. "I think the increase can be largely attributed to religious con-

servatives getting elected to school boards," she says. "It only takes one or two creationists on a school board to generate significant controversy, especially if the science curriculum undergoes periodic review."

Religious right groups like the Christian Coalition and Citizens for Excellence in Education have pushed hard to get right-wing Christians elected to local school boards in recent years. That's because school-board elections often elicit jaw-droppingly low voter turnout, making it easier for a small but motivated faction to elect its hand-picked candidate. School boards are also attractive to right-wingers because board members have — or at least appear to have — tremendous influence over what can and can't be taught in a community's schools.

Right-wing political activists also got a tremendous boost in 1994, when an electorate disenchanted with Bill Clinton voted an unprecedented number of Republicans into state-level and local offices. The legislatures in many states slid rightward literally overnight. Today, right-wing lawmakers are carrying out attacks on public

education on numerous fronts, with an eye toward pushing a fundamentalist political agenda — regardless of the wishes of most parents, teachers, and educators — and eroding the separation of church and state that has long been the hallmark of public schools. In addition to creationism, major battles are being waged around the country on such issues as school prayer, school-sponsored religious activity, so-called "parental-rights initiatives," sex education, and vouchers.

Carole Shields, president of People for the American Way, has called these attacks on public education "one element of the Right's attack on the fundamental institutions and values of American society. In attacking the schools, the Right is taking aim at the fundamental notion of opportunity for all. ... What better way to deny real opportunity could be devised than to hamper the institutions that furnish children with an education?"

Examples of creationists trying to use their political might to foist their religious beliefs on public schools include:

• In Vista, California, in 1992, voters elected a school board member who was also an accountant for the Institute for Creation Research. After the district's teachers rejected his suggestion to use the creationist book *Of Pandas and People* as a science textbook (see the story on page 40 for more on this book), he began advocating that teachers teach "weaknesses in evolution" whenever evolution was taught. Eventually, the board member and two others who had consistently voted with him on such issues were recalled.

• In Alabama in 1995, the state school board voted 6-1 in favor of a inserting a disclaimer into biology textbooks. Written by the right-wing Eagle Forum, it reads in part: "This textbook discusses evolution, a controversial theory some scientists present as a scientific explanation for the origin of living things. ... No one was present when life first appeared on earth. Therefore, any statement about life's origins should be considered as theory, not fact." According to People for the American Way, Alabama Governor Fob James, who is president of the state school board, urged the board to accept the motion, saying: "If one wanted to know some-

Jean-Claude Lejeune

thing about the origin of life you might want to look at Genesis and you can get the whole story, period." James also used his discretionary funds to purchase and send more than 900 copies of *Darwin on Trial*, a creationist book, to all biology teachers in the state.

• In Hall County, Georgia, in 1996, the school board adopted a resolution directing the textbook and curriculum committee to include materials in the science curriculum that explain and discuss creationism. The board rescinded this resolution after the state attorney general warned that this would be unconstitutional.

• In Tennessee in 1996, the Senate and House education committees both approved a bill that would have allowed schools to fire any teacher who presented evolution as a fact. A Senate amendment "defined" evolution as an "unproven belief that random, undirected forces produced a world of living things." Debate over the bill continued for months, despite an opinion issued by the state attorney general saying that the bill was unconstitutional. It was finally voted down by the Legislature.

Wesley Roberts, an ecology and environmental sciences teacher in Nashville, got himself — and his students — involved in the struggle to kill the Tennessee bill. He attended several sessions of the Legislature during the debates, sometimes bringing students from his school with him. "I think they (the students) were smart enough to realize that their teachers were about to be censored," he says, "and regardless of their position on creation and evolution, they did not like that at all." The students "definitely had an impact on the debate," he says. "The media were all over them, interviewing them. They loved getting sound bites from angry kids and plastering them all over TV and the newspaper."

While the rejection of the bill was "a real victory," Roberts says, it will take much more to really pave the way for evolution to be taught in Tennessee. Many teachers, mindful of all the ill will focused on evolution for so long, "won't even mention it in class," he says. Even students in his advanced-placement environ-

mental science class "have very rarely had any instruction in evolution." In fact, in a class Roberts teaches at a nearby college, "I always ask my students how much instruction they've had in evolution, and it's always the case that if they've had it, they went to a private school or they're from the North," he says.

This "chilling effect" stifles teachers all across the country, North as well as South. Even when creationists seem to lose a struggle, as in Tennessee, the controversy they generate can leave teachers wary to so much as mention evolution to their students. "There's a tendency for teachers to be noncombative," says Scott of the National Center for Science Education. "Generally teachers are not looking for a fight. ... If they perceive that a subject is going to get them in trouble, they may very well decide to just steer clear."

The Evolution of Creationism

Despite suffering some political and judicial setbacks, anti-evolutionists are not about to give up applying that pressure. Leaders of the creationist movement have been industrious and relatively skillful about repackaging and reintroducing their beliefs.

Take, for example, the creationists' response to the 1987 U.S. Supreme Court decision, known as Edwards vs. Aguillar, which struck down the Louisiana law requiring teachers to give equal time to "creation science" whenever they taught evolution. The late Justice William Brennan, writing the majority opinion, made it clear that "creation science" wasn't science at all, but an endorsement of faith-based religious belief. He also rejected the idea that the Louisiana law was promoting "a basic concept of fairness" by requiring that both evolution and creation science be taught. "Instead," he wrote, "this Act has the distinctly different purpose of discrediting evolution by counter-balancing its teaching at every turn with the teaching of creationism."

Brennan delivered a powerful rhetorical blow against anti-evolutionists. But deep in his 3,800-word opinion, creationists found a single sentence that gave them something they could build on. Bren-

nan had written: "Teaching a variety of scientific theories about the origins of humankind to schoolchildren might be validly done with the clear secular intent of enhancing the effectiveness of science instruction." And in the dissenting opinion by Justice Antonin Scalia, they found another useful phrase: "The people of Louisiana, including those who are Christian fundamentalists, are quite entitled, as a secular matter, to have whatever scientific evidence there may be against evolution presented in their schools ..."

These two statements set the stage for the two most current versions of creationism: the so-called "theory of intelligent design" and the efforts to inject "scientific evidence against evolution" into school curricula. Both are perhaps best exemplified by the creationist pseudo-textbook *Of Pandas and People*.

Similar reasoning lurks behind the many efforts to slap disclaimers on science textbooks, reminding students that evolution is "only a theory" and not fact. This is a serious misuse of the scientific meaning of "theory," making it sound like a synonym for "guess" or "hunch." In fact, according to the National Association of Biology Teachers, "a (scientific) theory is not a guess or an approximation, but an extensive explanation developed from well-documented, reproducible sets of experimentally derived data from repeated observations of natural processes." In other words, just because the theory of evolution is subject to continued testing and examination in light of new evidence doesn't make it untrue.

The reasons behind such attacks on evolution are obvious, according to a statement written by Rob Boston, a spokesman for the group Americans United for the Separation of Church and State. "They're shifting their attacks by trying to water down the teaching of evolution—put doubts in children's minds. They figure that if they can't get creationism taught in public schools, then the next best thing is to take the instruction about evolution and undercut it." ∎

Leon Lynn is a Milwaukee-based writer specializing in education issues. This article first appeared in *Rethinking Schools*, Winter 1997/1998 (Vol. 12, No. 2).

An interview with Scientist Eugenie Scott
What's a Teacher To Do?

Following is condensed from an interview with Eugenie Scott, executive director of the National Center for Science Education. Founded in 1981, the center supports teaching evolution and the separation of church and state. The center currently has about 3,500 members, including teachers, scientists, and activists advocating church-state separation.

Scott, who holds a doctorate in physical anthropology, has written articles about science education for numerous publications, including Natural History *and* The Scientist. *She was interviewed by Leon Lynn.*

How likely is it that a science teacher in this country will encounter creationism, or feel pressure for teaching evolution?

At some time or another in their career, very likely. It varies based on where they work, of course. Usually, teachers in big cities will fare better than teachers in small towns and suburbs. But it's a common thing, and it seems to be getting more common.

There are two sides to this. One is the effort by creationists to teach some kind of religiously based idea as part of the science curriculum. That's usually pretty blatant. But there's another side, which can be a lot harder to see. Teachers get the message, sometimes overtly, sometimes more subtly, that evolution has become a controversial subject in their community and they'll just quietly stop teaching it, and evolution will sink out of the curriculum.

How do you respond when someone

suggests that the fair thing to do is teach children about both evolution and creationism, and let them decide what to believe?

At its heart, the "equal-time" argument is substantially flawed. People who advocate it are basically saying we should teach that evolutionary theory — the idea that the universe changed through time, that the present is different from past — is equal in weight to the idea that the whole universe came into being at one time and hasn't changed since then. You can't do that in a science class. You can only deal with scientific evidence. There is copious evidence to support that evolution has occurred, and no evidence that everything was created at once and hasn't changed. Why would we pretend that an idea that was created outside of science is science? That's not fair.

It's perfectly reasonable to expose children to religious views of origin, but it's not OK to advocate those views as empirical truth. And the place for those ideas is not in the science curriculum.

Do you think students are harmed by exposure to creationism in their science class?

Yes. To begin with, these so-called alternatives to evolution are disadvantageous because they are simply factually wrong. Creation science literature is riddled with inaccuracies, misstatements. Students who learn it learn a lot of flat-out erroneous stuff. They also aren't learning the scientific method. The people pushing

creation science aren't interested in modifying or revisiting their theories based on any new evidence, which is the basic premise of science. So when you teach creation science, you're giving legitimacy to very bad scholarship.

It's also a problem for students because if they don't learn evolution, they will be at a disadvantage when they take standardized tests. That includes college admissions tests. Evolution is not controversial at the college level. Scientists who work and teach at that level constantly tell me how amazed they are at the ignorance of students about evolution.

When teachers feel pressure to stop teaching evolution, what should they do?

To begin with, it's important to deal with people's feelings. If a religious parent is raising a complaint, for example, it's very important to make that parent realize you're not trying to change or challenge the child's religious faith. You need to say, "We are presenting the best scientific information, we want your children to learn it, but it's up to you and them whether they accept it or not." That often assuages parents' concern, because they're really afraid that when evolution is being taught, anti-religious ideas are being rammed down their children's throats.

Also, teachers need to support each other. If there are teachers in your school who are nervous about teaching evolution, others need to support them. Those teachers need to know they're not alone in

> *The people pushing creation science aren't interested in modifying or revisiting their theories based on any new evidence, which is the basic premise of science.*

case any flak comes along.

And probably the most important thing for teachers to do is to get administrative support. That is, if they can.

What do you mean?

I've heard some great stories of administrators marching into the classroom and saying, "You will teach evolution, you signed a contract to teach the curriculum and that's part of it." I'd sure like to clone them, though, because we sure don't have many like that. I've been rather disappointed on the whole with the response of principals. The proper response in a situation like that is to explain to the parent the importance of evolution in the school curriculum. Instead, too many principals tend to appease the parent by talking to the teacher, and directing the teacher to "just skip it (evolution) this year." I've had teachers tell me stories like that at every conference I've ever attended.

Administrators are simply not doing their jobs on this. If a parent came in and said, "I don't want my child learning that the South lost the civil war," the principal would say, "Thanks for your input, but we have to teach the curriculum, including the part that says the North won." Or if you had a parent who was a Holocaust revisionist, you wouldn't see many principals telling teachers to stop teaching that the Holocaust took place. But they're willing to compromise the integrity of science and tell the teachers to downplay or skip evolution.

Why is evolution treated differently?

The difference is partly due to people not wanting to be critical of religion. Administrators don't want to be labeled as being "anti-God." Remember, there are a lot of people who think that when you accept evolution, you have to reject religion. That's not true, but there are an awful lot of administrators who would rather just avoid the whole issue than start a debate like that with parents.

Another part of it is that there's a lot of ignorance among administrators about the central importance of evolution to science teaching. They don't realize that evolution is a central, unifying theory of biology, and that depriving students of learning it is a serious problem. ■

National Academy of Sciences

"There is no debate within the scientific community over whether evolution has occurred, and there is no evidence that evolution has not occurred."
— *National Academy of Sciences*

The National Academy of Sciences has issued a guidebook to bolster the teaching of evolution, calling it "the most important concept to modern biology."

"There is no debate within the scientific community over whether evolution has occurred, and there is no evidence that evolution has not occurred," according to the academy.

In a report released April 9, 1998, the academy said that many students "receive little or no exposure" to evolution, and expressed dismay that some teachers avoid evolution for fear of reprisals from fundamentalists religious groups. In Arizona, for example, the Board of Education kept the word "evolution" out of the state biology standards. Similar efforts are underway in several other states.

The academy noted that "teaching biology without evolution would be like teaching civics and never mentioning the United States Constitution."

Bruce Alberts, the academy's president, said that more teachers "are reluctant to teach" about the central concept of evolution because of pressure from religious fundamentalist groups. He said the academy's hope is that the new guide will help teachers who want to teach evolution.

The National Academy of Sciences is a non-profit group chartered by the U.S. Congress to give the nation guidance on important scientific matters. School districts are not required to accept the academy's advice, but science teachers believe the academy provides useful curricular materials. Teachers will find especially helpful their new book, *Teaching About Evolution and the Nature of Science* ($19.95).

Also available is a 32-page booklet, *Science and Creationism* ($7.95), from the National Academy Press, call 1-800-624-6242.

For more information visit the academy's web page: www.nap.edu/readingroom/books/evolution98. ■

Controversy Strikes a School District

One Town's Battle Over Creationism

by Leon Lynn

Andrew Aljancic is persistent. It's been more than seven years since he started actively campaigning against the teaching of evolution in the public schools of Louisville, Ohio. Two years ago, he even left his seat on the town council and successfully ran for the school board in hopes of furthering his agenda.

Aljancic has pushed repeatedly for the inclusion of so-called "creation science" in the district's science curricula. He's tried to get the school district to adopt the creationist treatise *Of Pandas and People* as a science textbook. He wants the district's science curricula to include creation-science doctrine and he's also hoping to get disclaimer stickers plastered into biology and life-science textbook which call evolution "a controversial theory."

Fortunately, James Bollas is persistent too. A 70-year-old retired teacher, whose five children and four grandchildren graduated from Louisville schools, Bollas is a self-described political conservative who has a fondness for the U.S. Constitution. He's outraged at the thought of "someone using my tax dollars to teach their religion in the public schools." And he won't accept any effort to include creationist materials in the school's curricula. He's been a fixture at Louisville school board meetings for years, using the designated public-comment time to speak against the various anti-evolution resolutions the board has considered.

Bollas doesn't recall a single occasion when anyone else has stood up at a school board meeting to agree with him. But that hasn't stopped him from speaking his mind and from calling in the American Civil Liberties Union to help keep the school district in compliance with the law.

As is often the case in skirmishes over constitutional rights such as the separation of church and state, it can be a lonely

battle. Constitutional principles are revered more in theory than in practice and many people fail to adequately understand that the very heart of the Bill of Rights involves protecting constitutional rights even when the majority in a locale or state may disagree.

"The problem is that most of the people in Louisville agree on creationism," Bollas says. "It's what they believe and so they don't have a problem with seeing it in the schools. The Constitution and the Bill of Rights say they can't do that, that it's wrong, but in Louisville nobody seems to know about that, or maybe nobody wants to know. So I consider it my job to keep reminding them."

"A Community of Nice Folks"

The small Midwestern town of Louisville provides a concrete example of how issues such as creationism often play out in our nation's schools. Located about 10 miles northeast of Canton in the rolling farmland of Ohio's Stark County, Louisville (pronounced LEWIS-ville) is home to about 8,000 people. The virtually all-white community includes farmers, people who work at the few local factories, and many who commute to jobs in Canton and other nearby communities. The Louis-

ville school system — four elementary schools, a middle school, and a high school — serves about 3,100 students from the town and the surrounding area.

"It's a community of nice folks," says James Warner, another Louisville school board member. "Close-knit, basically conservative." Warner, who has served on the board for 12 years, says evolution has long been an issue in Louisville. In 1986, the district's science curriculum directed teachers to "contrast, compare and discuss alternatives to the evolutionary theory, particularly creationism." This was before a 1987 U.S. Supreme Court decision which struck down a Louisiana requirement that creationism receive the same attention as evolution in school curricula. The directive was later withdrawn, Warner says, after the ACLU threatened to sue the district, but the curriculum still directed teachers to present "alternatives to evolutionary theory."

The evolution issue became more prominent in Louisville in about 1990 when Aljancic, as leader of a local fundamentalist group called the Origins Committee, began pressing the district to include more creationist material in the curriculum. Originally from Cleveland, Aljancic has lived in Louisville for most of his 55 years. He teaches English and speech at a local Catholic school, though his own children have all attended the town's public schools.

Aljancic says he grew up in "kind of a borderline Catholic family." Today he believes in the inerrancy of the Bible, and that Christianity "is really the only faith that answers the questions of life, why we die, and how we can live again." He also believes that the theory of evolution "is in contradiction with the Bible" and that if students are taught only evolution they'll accept it "because that's all they'll know." Like many creationists, he puts forth the "theory of intelligent design," the supposedly secular idea that life is too complex and remarkable to have sprung up purely by chance.

Aljancic asked the school district to start using the controversial book *Of Pandas and People* as a science text (see the story on page 45). He and the Origins Committee even raised $13,000 to help defray the costs of any legal challenges the district encountered over the book. When the district refused — officially because *Pandas* is not on Ohio's list of acceptable textbooks — the Origins Committee bought 100 copies of the book and donated them to the school district to be used as a supplemental text and reference.

Ongoing Skirmishes

Since joining the board two years ago,

How has this ongoing controversy over evolution affected the school district? To begin with, Lepley thinks some teachers, fearing for their jobs, simply avoid teaching evolution at all.

Aljancic has "pushed a very focused agenda, all about public schools getting more value-oriented, more traditional," says Clyde Lepley, the Louisville district's superintendent. "I think he'd like to see more religion in our schools. ..."Creationism remains at the heart of that agenda, Lepley believes, but he says Aljancic "has backed off a bit" in light of the legal restrictions and the rules of decorum that the district and its board members must follow.

But the struggle continues. Last November, for example, the five-member school board unanimously passed a resolution that "scientific evidence both for and against evolution" should be presented whenever evolution is taught. This summer, when the district presented the board with the science curriculum for the coming year, Aljancic objected. "They were treating evolution as fact," he says. "There was no other side at all. They were basically ignoring the (November) resolution."

Aljancic even wanted the board to vote on whether the section on evolution should be deleted from the curriculum. But during the meeting the board president, Mark Sigler, "asked me if I trust the superintendent and the curriculum director," Aljancic says. "I agreed that I did, and so I withdrew my amendments." The board then approved the science curriculum 3-2, with Aljancic and Warner dissenting. The district's curriculum officials, in turn, have agreed to examine a list of Aljancic's "pros and cons" on evolution and decide whether any of them warrant inclusion in the district's course of study.

Also this summer, Aljancic asked the board to adopt the Alabama science-book stickers. His motion died for lack of a second but Warner predicts the sticker question will come up another time.

The Damage Done

How has this ongoing controversy over evolution affected the school district? To begin with, Lepley thinks some teachers, fearing for their jobs, simply avoid teaching evolution at all. "I do think some of them are afraid," he says. "There's so much content in biology, you could really let that go and move on, so I think that the easier road to take here is not get into that at all."

Overall, Lepley says, "I think this is

Retired teacher James Bollas speaks out against anti-evolution proposals.

Paul Tople

having a negative effect on the school district. ... It's continually putting the board off course. We've got teacher negotiations we're going through right now, we're trying to do a facilities study, and see what our needs are going to be for the next century. This issue is taking the focus away from that. It's not just the time spent on it, but it's an overriding cloud that everybody's always thinking about."

Lepley also suspects that Aljancic has other plans. "My job is to keep the board out of the courts, I've tried to keep them out of trouble," he says. "I'm not so sure Mr. Aljancic thinks that's appropriate. I think he thinks he can win, that Louisville can be a leader of the pack, a shining star."

Raymond Vasvari tends to agree. A Cleveland-area lawyer who volunteers his time to the American Civil Liberties Union, Vasvari has kept an eye on Louisville since 1993. He started following events there after Bollas complained to the ACLU about the board's pro-creationist activities. "I've been calling it the test case that wants to be," Vasvari says. "The people there seem determined to start

something." Several times since 1993, Vasvari has written letters to the Louisville school board on the ACLU's behalf, threatening legal action over pro-creationist policies.

Vasvari believes that the situation in Louisville is part of a national, often times orchestrated push for creationism and for breaking down the separation of church and state. He also believes that many town residents don't understand the full implications of the controversy, and are therefore unable to adequately ward off the agenda of people such as Aljancic. "I really don't think the situation is ever going to be resolved without someone coming in from outside, like the courts," Bollas says. He adds that there are plenty of people in Louisville "who are doctors and lawyers, who know something about the world. But they aren't getting involved in the schools. They aren't at the meetings. Maybe they don't care, or maybe they're afraid to stand up. I'm the only one who opposes them" (the creationists).

A big part of the problem is that a lot of people in Louisville agree with Aljancic

about creationism. "It doesn't matter to them what the Constitution says, or what science says," Bollas says. "What matters is what they believe, and that they all believe the same thing. It's hard for outsiders to understand. But in the town, there's no one to challenge them, no one who's willing to stand up for anything different. I can understand it though. Most of the people here in town would say you're either a creationist or an atheistic evolutionist. That can be pretty hard to take."

Bollas laughs. "I guess my problem is that I'm an idealistic old man. But I believe in the Constitution. I believe in the Bill of Rights. And I won't just sit there and watch them push their religion into the schools. It's not just me against Andy Aljancic. It's me against all those people who would take away my citizenship." ∎

This article first appeared in *Rethinking Schools*, Winter 1997/1998 (Vol. 12, No. 2).

Louisville (Ohio) school board members.

Paul Tople

Creationists Push Pseudo-Science Text

With its glossy cover, full-color illustrations, and chapter titles like "Homology" and "Genetics and Macroevolution," *Of Pandas and People* sure looks like a science textbook, and a classy one at that. But get past the flashy packaging and start digging into the text and it soon becomes clear that it's not. *Of Pandas and People* is a creationist treatise dressed up to look like a legitimate discussion of science.

Pandas is published by a group called the Foundation for Thought and Ethics, based in the Dallas suburb of Richardson. Advocates of creationism have tried to get *Pandas* adopted as a state textbook in Idaho, Alabama, and Texas, and pro-creationism school board members have sought its local adoption in numerous school districts, including Vista, CA and Louisville, OH (See story on Louisville, page 42). Conservative groups such as Concerned Women for America and Citizens for Excellence in Education have championed *Pandas*, portraying it as a factual scientific analysis that tears gaping holes in the theory of evolution.

Pandas claims to offer evidence for the so-called "theory of intelligent design." Simply put, "intelligent design" is the belief that life is so complex and remarkable that it could not have developed without an intelligent, purposeful guiding hand. According to the book:

When we find "John loves Mary" written in the sand, we assume it resulted from an intelligent cause. Experience is the basis for science as well. When we find a complex message coded into the nucleus of a cell, it is reasonable to draw the same conclusion. ... To say that DNA and protein arose by natural causes, as chemical evolution does, is to say complex, coded messages arose by natural causes. It is akin to saying "John loves Mary" arose from the action of the waves, or from the interaction of the grains of sand. It is like saying the painting of a sunset arose spontaneously from the atoms in the paint and canvas.

The identity of the "designer" is never specifically discussed, thus providing creationists with grounds to claim, however transparently, that *Pandas* isn't arguing for the existence of God or promoting a religious view. The 170-page book claims to present data from different scientific disciplines which discredit evolution and support the "scientific rationale" behind intelligent design. Page after page of professionally prepared charts and illustrations appear to show how concrete scientific evidence supports the existence of the unnamed "designer."

The emphasis is on presenting intelligent design as a legitimate scientific theory, one that's at least as credible as the theory of evolution. Readers, presumably students, are told in the book's introduction that if they don't read *Pandas*, "you would miss a lot of interesting science." The introduction also says that the authors hope readers "finish this book respecting good scientists of all persuasions; we do."

A lot of good scientists, however, don't have any respect for *Of Pandas and People*. Michael Ruse, a professor of philosophy and zoology at the University of Guelph in Ontario, Canada, termed the book "worthless and dishonest" in a 1989 review. Kevin Padian, a paleontologist at the University of California-Berkeley and one of the authors of the science framework for California's schools, called Pandas "a wholesale distortion of modern biology." He said: "It is hard to say what is worst in this book: the misconceptions of its sub-text, the intolerance for honest science, or the incompetence with which science is presented. In any case, teachers should be warned against using this book."

Gerald R. Skoog, an education professor at Texas Tech University, a former biology teacher and a past president of the National Science Teachers Association, has a similarly low opinion of *Pandas,* saying; "It's just not science." Even if you gloss over inaccuracies and misrepresentations of scientific theory in *Pandas*, he says, "the claim that life is the result of

Andrew Aljancic of Louisville, Ohio, (see story page 42) holds Of Pandas and People.

intelligent design can't be tested by scientific means, and it has no power to explain the natural world."

While *Pandas* claims to be a science book, it's really a political tool, says Raymond Vasvari, a lawyer in Ohio who works with the American Civil Liberties Union and who has been involved in issues involving creationism. "I call *Of Pandas and People* the intellectual Trojan horse of the religious right," Vasvari says. "It looks and feels and acts like a science textbook, but it's not. It's a message aimed at the seventh-grader who doesn't know science or understand the controversy over evolution and creationism." ∎

Resources on Evolution and Creationism

BOOKS FOR ADULTS

Berra, Tim M. *Evolution and the Myth of Creationism* (Stanford: Stanford University Press, 1990). A concise, readable 200-page guide to the theory of evolution and some of the creationists' common objections. A good reference for the non-scientist.

Gould, Stephen Jay, *Bully for Brontosaurus: Reflections in Natural History* (New York: Norton, 1991).

Gould, Stephen Jay, *Dinosaur in a Haystack: Reflections in Natural History* (New York: Harmony Books, 1995).

Both of these books by the popular Harvard paleontologist give the reader a digestible dose of sophisticated evidence supporting evolutionary theory, and the attempts by religious fundamentalists to twist that evidence to support their own claims. *Bully for Brontosaurus* in particular provides a revealing history of the objections raised by anti-evolutionists.

BOOKS FOR CHILDREN

Cole, Joanna. *The Human Body: How We Evolved* (New York: William Morrow and Co., 1987). Traces the development of humans from early prehistoric ancestors to the modern-tool user who walks upright. 3rd grade/up.

Sattler, Helen Roney. *Hominids: A Look Back At Our Ancestors* (New York, Lothrop, Lee & Shepard, 1988). Describes through line drawings and text the various hominids which preceded Homo Sapiens, as deduced from fossil remains. 5th grade and up.

Stein, Sara. *The Evolution Book* (New York: Workman Publishing Co., 1986). A 390 page book bursting with experiments, investigations, projects and pictures that show readers how to unlock the wonders of nature and evolution. 5th grade and up.

ASSOCIATIONS

Americans United for Separation of Church and State, 1816 Jefferson Place NW, Washington, DC 20036. 202-466-3234; fax 202-466-2587. e-mail: americansunited@au.org; Web site: www.au.org.

Founded in 1947, Americans United for Separation of Church and State is a nonpartisan, nonprofit educational organization promoting the principle of church-state separation as an essential constitutional guarantee of religious liberty.

The National Association of Biology Teachers, 11250 Roger Bacon Drive, #19, Reston, VA 20190-5202. 703-471-1134 or 800-406-0775; fax 703-435-5582. e-mail: office@nabt.org; Web site: www.nabt.org.

The largest national association of biology and life-science educators, with more than 7,000 members. It offers position papers and resources on a variety of issues, including the teaching of evolution.

The National Center for Science Education, PO Box 9477, Berkeley, CA 94709-0477. 510-526-1674 or 800-290-6006; fax 510-526-1675. e-mail: ncse@NatCenSciEd.org; Web site: www.natcenscied.org.

The National Center for Science Education supports the teaching of evolution and keeping religious views that masquerade as science out of the classroom. It offers a variety of resources including publications, workshops, expert testimony for school board hearings, and advice on how to organize for political action.

National Committee for Public Education and Religious Liberty (PEARL), PO Box 586, FDR Station, New York, NY 10150. 212-486-4590.

A coalition of 55 member groups, ranging from the Baptist Joint Committee to the National Education Association and the National Council of Jewish Women, committed to keeping church and state separate in school systems and to maintaining public schools as safe havens for people of all creeds. PEARL focuses on litigation.

The National Science Teachers Association, 1840 Wilson Blvd., Arlington, VA 22201-3000. 703-243-7100. Web site: www.nsta.org.

The largest science-teaching organization, with more than 53,000 members. Produces a wide variety of publications for children and adults, and provides programs and services for science educators, including professional certification for science teachers in eight teaching level and discipline area categories. Its position paper on evolution includes detailed curriculum recommendations.

People for the American Way, 2000 M. St., NW, Suite 400, Washington, DC 20006. 202-467-4999. e-mail: pfaw@pfaw.org; Web site: www.pfaw.org.

Probably the best single source of information on the religious right, this group publishes a variety of reports.

The Institute for Creation Research, 10946 Woodside Ave., North Santee, CA 92071. 619-448-0900; fax 619-448-3469.Web site: www.icr.org.

One of the most vocal and prolific organizations promoting creationism and attacking evolution, ICR puts forth the position that "all genuine facts of science support the Bible," and states its mission as "to see science return to its rightful God-glorifying position." A very candid and comprehensive look at what creationists believe and what they seek to accomplish.

ALSO ON THE WORLD WIDE WEB
The Talk.Origins Archive Web site: www.talkorigins.org.

The archive is an outgrowth of the talk.origins Usenet newsgroup, where discussions focus on the creation/evolution struggle and related science topics. It includes a tremendous volume of material on the scientific basis of evolutionary theory and those who seek to discredit it, arranged in a very accessible fashion. ■

GAY ISSUES

Affirming the "Public" in Public Education

Gay Issues, Schools, and the Right-wing Backlash

by Eric Rofes

In Colorado Springs, home to powerful right-wing organizations and the U.S. Air Force Academy, the Palmer High School student newspaper writes a front-page story on the problems confronting lesbian and gay youth. An editorial supports same-sex marriage.

The far right Concerned Women of America (CWA) meanwhile launches a campaign against the National Education Association for promotion of homosexuality and "imposition of immoral values." School boards throughout the country are asked to promote a CWA "Pro-family Resolution."

Across the United States, and not just in urban areas such as New York or Los Angeles, the issue of sexual orientation and schools has become a major controversy. Sometimes, lesbian/gay/bisexual students are at the forefront of the issue. Sometimes, far-right organizations are setting the agenda.

Is anyone "winning" this cultural war? And why have the public schools emerged as such an important battlefield in the fight for the rights of gays and lesbians? Furthermore, how do such issues relate to the broader struggle over the future of public education in this country?

Easy answers to such questions are elusive. As a starting point, however, consider the astounding new documentary *It's Elementary, Talking About Gay Issues in Schools*, by Debra Chasnoff and Helen Cohen.

In the documentary, first graders write stories about gay and lesbian families, third graders discuss same-sex marriage, and middle school students learn that gay people come from all racial and ethnic groups. Teachers, parents, and principals discuss the best way to include gay and lesbian issues in elementary school curricula and debate whether the aim is to

Students demonstrated in Salt Lake City against the school board when it eliminated extracurricular clubs rather than allow a support group for gay and lesbian students.

Paul Barker/Deseret News

"teach tolerance" or to "value diversity." One school even initiates a schoolwide celebration of Lesbian and Gay Pride, complete with pink triangle buttons and presentations from openly gay teachers.

Kaylin, a second grade student, reads a story she wrote about marching in her hometown's gay pride parade.

Kaylin was in the march saying, "Hey, hey. Ho, ho. Homophobia's got to go."

She then writes how homophobia "means being scared of gay or lesbian people." In a picture to accompany the story, the crowd is also chanting, "Hey, hey. Ho, ho. Homophobia's got to go."

The documentary serves as a 1990s testimony to the ways lesbian and gay issues are becoming integrated into everyday life in some public and private schools in the United States. By collecting film footage of young children making sense of homosexuality and grappling with the discrimination and bigotry faced by lesbians, gay men, and bisexuals, the filmmakers provide a powerful refutation to the right's "children can't deal with homosexuality" rhetoric.

Chasnoff and Cohen aren't satisfied with the liberal compromise which kept gay issues pigeonholed as the purview of high school teachers and health classes. They show that gay issues are ubiquitous in the lives of children — from television talk shows and movies aimed at children, to playground slurs and hallway graffiti. They insist that the reality of children's lives be confronted in classroom pedagogy.

Yet most educators — gay, lesbian,

bisexual, or heterosexual — who are grappling with these issue do not teach in the large urban centers (New York and San Francisco) or liberal college towns (Cambridge or Madison) featured in *It's Elementary*. They work in places like Salt Lake City, Utah, Elizabethtown, Penn., or Colorado Springs, Colo. Lesbian and gay issues play out very differently in these locations than they do in San Francisco or Madison. Consider:

• In response to the formation of a gay-straight alliance to provide peer support to lesbian, gay, and bisexual youth at Salt Lake City's East High School, the school board banned all student clubs and associations not formally tied to school curricula. Banished are groups ranging from hockey and mountain bike clubs, to Native American and Polynesian associations, to the school's Key Club.

• Inspired by a "pro-family" resolution drafted by Beverly LeHaye, president of Concerned Women of America, the school board of Elizabethtown, Penn., adopted a resolution condemning various family forms — including single-parent families, extended families, and lesbian and gay

families. Despite student walkouts and community-wide protests, the board has refused to reconsider its position. It recently proposed an expanded anti-gay policy stating that "the curriculum will not promote or encourage same-sex sexual relationships or orientation." The board has received support from both Concerned Women of America and the Rutherford Institute, a far-right legal advocacy group.

• In October, 1996, the Palmer High School newspaper included two student-initiated articles about gay issues, a front-page story on the trials facing lesbian and gay youth in a hostile culture, and an editorial supporting same-sex marriage. Immediately after publication, the local Christian right mounted a campaign demanding tighter controls on student publications. Colorado for Family Values, the group which initiated the state's controversial anti-gay initiative (later declared unconstitutional by the U.S. Supreme Court), jumped into the fray. Their effort is focused on getting school boards to "promote abstinence, affirm traditional marriage, and discourage promiscuity ... in every aspect of student life."

Teachers Network Jumps to the Forefront

Founded in 1990 as a local, Massachusetts-based group, in the past seven years the Gay, Lesbian, and Straight Education Network (GLSEN) has grown into a national organization with over 80 local chapters and almost 10,000 members.

Founder and executive director Kevin Jennings told *Rethinking Schools* that in 1990 the group "had no conception that fighting the religious right would be a primary focus for us." But since then, GLSEN has been front and center of most of the key conflicts involving lesbian and gay issues in the schools. Whether coming up against the Traditional Values Coalition, Concerned Women of America, Eagle Forum, or the Christian Coalition, GLSEN activists often comprise the frontline in battles to keep public education accessible to all students.

Jennings insists the group makes a de-

liberate attempt to remain "pro-active rather than reactive." He said that GLSEN organizers understand that the right-wing's strategy is to try to create as many localized points of conflict as possible in order to keep progressive organizers in constant crisis mode.

GLSEN resisted this reactive mode most directly when the Concerned Women of America launched a national campaign against GLSEN and its Gay History Month campaign, as well as the National Education Association which had voted to support the campaign.

As part of the pro-active emphasis, GLSEN is launching a School Board Organizing Project to get chapters more involved in local electoral politics. The group hopes to develop a "progressive report card" and rate school board candidates on issues which are of local concern. Jen-

nings says GLSEN's aim is to "build unity among different groups" who are concerned with "keeping public schools accessible to every child in the community."

Jennings argues that the right wing "gets reactionaries onto school boards, then pushes prayer in schools and creationism. It's almost like a Trojan horse — they use gay issues to get into the schools and pursue a larger agenda." ■

GLSEN organizes local conferences and leadership training programs throughout the nation and produces videos, posters, school materials, staff development resources, and other publications.

GLSEN can be reached at 121 W. 27th St., Suite 804, New York, NY 10011. 212-727-0135; fax 212-727-0254; e-mail: GLSEN.org; website: www.GLSEN.org.

— *Eric Rofes*

Donna Binder/Impact Visuals

New York City high school students protest neglect of the concerns of lesbian and gay students.

Paradoxical Position

This is a tumultuous time for social justice advocates working on making schools safe for lesbian, gay, bisexual, and transgender youth and for teachers committed to serving all their students. Never before has so much activity emerged in public schools which challenges educators, school boards, and communities to come to terms with issues which were unimaginable 25 years ago, except for in a few key urban centers. Issues span a broad spectrum: openly gay and lesbian teachers and principals, out-of-the-closet students who are organizing for their rights, lesbian mothers leading PTAs, explicit sex education and AIDS prevention curricula which deal head-on with gay male sexuality. The National Education Association offers a resolution in 1995 supporting Gay, Lesbian, and Bisexual History Month. The American Educational Research Association holds a special day-long training at its 1996 annual meeting for researchers whose

work focuses on gay issues in schools. Courses on anti-homophobia education and gay issues in education pop up at Education Schools such as Berkeley and Harvard.

Yet never before have gay issues in schools been the target of such a multitude of local, statewide, and national efforts by a highly-organized right wing. In Anchorage, Alaska, the school board was forced to vote last fall on whether a gay/straight alliance might remain active on a high school campus. In Idaho, the state superintendent of public instruction threatened this winter to return $80,000 in federal funding for HIV/AIDS education, insisting on an "abstinence only" policy which effectively writes off gay male youth as an expendable population. In Modesto, Calif., anti-gay organizers launched an attack on teachers planning to attend a regional conference on gay issues in schools in the spring of 1996 and insisted that no district funds be used for this kind of staff

development.

It is easy to feel overwhelmed with the current volume and intensity of attacks on gay and lesbian participation in public schools. On a weekly basis, teachers have their jobs threatened for including gay issues in their classrooms, students feel increasingly marginalized by their peers, and books are eliminated from libraries.

Yet this is also a time of impressive progress and important opportunities. This January, Arizona state officials considered proposing a ban to outlaw gay student clubs from their schools; the same month, Massachusetts saw the founding of its 100th public-school-based gay-straight alliance. A few weeks after an Arkansas youth was harassed and viciously attacked in an anti-gay campaign by his peers last fall, Jamie Nabozny, a young gay man from Wisconsin, won nearly $1 million in damages from his high school for failing to protect him from years of peer abuse. During a time when 52% of school board members in the United States identify themselves as religious conservatives, the *Harvard Educational Review*, arguably the nation's leading journal on academic research, published a special issue (Summer 1996) focused on gay, lesbian, and bisexual issues in schools.

Uneven Progress

The current political landscape on gay/lesbian school issues feels like a paradox because many of us have been inculcated in a simplistic, linear model of social change. We believe that political organizing has a specific trajectory of wins and losses which eventually culminates in total victory. Yet the past 30 years of organizing in various movements has made it clear that a more dynamic and less predictable pattern of victories and defeats, backlashes, and retreats, surprise gains and disappointing losses are mixed together in the social change stew.

Thus it's not surprising that as gay is-

Kellie Peterson, left, with a friend at a Board of Education meeting.

sues have moved from invisible (1960), to socially marginal (1970), to part of a "liberal agenda" (1980), to a central place in mainstream political debate (1990s), the anti-gay right wing has shifted tactics and re-energized and reinvented its attacks. In the 20 years since Anita Bryant and California Senator John Briggs first brought gay issues in schools into the public debate, both the right wing and the gay and lesbian movement have increased in sophistication, resources, and organizational know-how. Hence the skirmishes occur with increasingly higher visibility and increasingly higher stakes.

Peter LaBarbara, a leading figure of the religious right, summarized the right wing's understanding of attempts by advocates for gay and lesbian youth and teachers to make schools safe for all. In prepared remarks for a recent Capitol Hill briefing in support of the anti-gay Defense of Marriage Act, LaBarbara wrote:

"The campaign to teach school children and teens that 'gay is OK' benefits from the usual coordination of a united 'gay' movement which has the advantage of pressing for a single radical goal, versus its pro-family opponents who face a multiplicity of challenges. Parents who simply want a good education for their children are increasingly confronted with the prospect of seeing precious educational resources spent on talking about homosexuality, and they are drawn into time-consuming and divisive debates over this issue."

Are teachers, parents, and administrators who aim to "do the right thing" for lesbian and gay students, simply pawns in a greater "campaign" organized around what LaBarbara calls "a single radical goal"? Is it possible for educators to be both committed to a "good education" and believe that frank, respectful discussion of lesbian and gay issues is part of quality education? How can the right wing simultaneously be leading efforts to limit and in some cases reduce public funding for schools and blaming "talking about homosexuality" for limiting the financial resources available for education?

Gay Issues as Wedge Issues

Suzanne Pharr, in her powerful new book, *In the Time of the Right: Reflections on Liberation*, argues that the issue of homosexuality "provided a major source of fundraising for the Right's organizations as well as their best vehicle for changing the country's thinking about civil rights." She also notes that homosexuality has effectively functioned as a "wedge" issue.

Pharr shows how homophobia is used to divide and fragment communities of color, "destroy the potential for multi-issue movement building," and allow the right wing to gain a toe-hold in new spheres where it can then launch campaigns for its broader and more far-reaching agenda.

The right wing's attack on public schooling offers one of the best examples of how gay issues are used as a front to amass support in preparation for a larger agenda. It has been relatively easy for right-wing organizers to garner mass support and raise big bucks when gay issues can be fanned into a local sex panic. They've successfully done this in circumstances ranging from a gay teacher getting "married" to a same sex partner, to the introduction of Gay, Lesbian, and Bisexual History Month as a curricular feature, to AIDS groups offering prevention education for youth in schools. Skillful organizing by right-wing activists deploys stereotyping and scapegoating as weapons intended to encourage citizens to channel a range of anxieties and misgivings — about their local schools but even about extraneous non-school issues — into triggering the gay issue.

This has frequently brought about the election of religious right activists to local boards of education, the banning of books and other educational materials, and an escalating public rhetoric of "family values." Yet, once in power, a much broader agenda emerges as the true game plan.

Lesbians and gay men continue to be marginalized and scapegoated, but broader philosophical and pedagogical questions swiftly emerge: elimination of all sex education, opposition to pedagogies intended to strengthen critical thinking, attacks on the teaching of whole language, considerations of expanded privatization of schooling, challenges to multicultural history units. The right wing pushes forward to support expanded and deregulated home schooling, voucher initiatives that would include parochial schools, the teaching of creationism rather than evolution, and an exclusive focus on phonics in the teaching of reading.

The interaction between this broad agenda attacking public education and lesbian and gay issues is evident in a recent video produced by Eagle Forum and hosted by Phyllis Schlafly. Entitled *Crisis in the Classroom*, the hour-long video seems designed to serve as a wake-up call to parents throughout America who must immediately organize and take back public education from the unions, socialists, and queers. The film purports to show how the misguided thinking of "socialist" philosophers such as Hegel and John Dewey has squirreled its way into a dominant position in public schools. It then goes on to attack cooperative learning, outcome-based education, and whole-language instruction — arguing that such pedagogical perspectives are part of a plot by the "educational establishment" (read, "the unions") to take over the minds of the young.

Thus far in the video, there is nary a peep about gay issues. Yet at the climax of the video, a mother who organized in Alabama to keep Goals 2000 money out of the state — because it would force the schools to abandon phonics-only teaching methods and to adhere to federal education guidelines focused on equity — begins raving about a "lesbian counselor with an agenda" at her child's school. This then turns into a larger discussion of how schools are channeling funds into "teaching homosexuality" and "showing movies of people having sex," rather than into traditional classroom teaching methods.

While gay issues make only a brief cameo appearance in this Eagle Forum video, they are positioned to hook viewers into accepting a much broader right-wing critique of education.

Who's Fighting the Right?

The heroes in the public battles to address lesbian and gay issues in schools tend to be ordinary individuals who stand

Gay father with son at 1992 protest in New York City supporting the inclusion of gay and lesbian issues in the curriculum.

Linda Eber/Impact Visuals

up to the bigotry and bullying tactics of the right wing. Most do not start off considering themselves social justice advocates or politically savvy strategists. They seem to hold a common commitment to public education and a broad understanding of how what is considered "the public" is under constant attack these days.

When a rural New Hampshire school administrator attempted to keep gay-themed books out of high school English classes, she unwisely chose to target Penny Culliton. A heterosexual teacher with tremendous integrity, Culliton believed that gay issues merited examination in the schools. She decided to continue to teach such books, was fired, and successfully fought her firing in the courts.

In Wisconsin, meanwhile, when school officials in Ashland spent three years looking the other way as a teenage boy was scapegoated, bullied, and beaten by his peers, they didn't know they were dealing with Jamie Nabozny. With support from his family, Nabozny filed a ground-break-

ing lawsuit arguing that school officials bear responsibility for ensuring that homosexual students are not subjected to abuse and harassment.

When the Salt Lake City School Board took radical action to keep young gays and lesbians from creating a support group with the schools, they forgot about the Kellie Petersons of the world. A newly "out" lesbian teenager in the school, Peterson would successfully lobby, protest, and organize to create and sustain such a group — and in the process focused national attention on what, until then, had seemed just another local school controversy.

The right wing argues that there is a vast conspiracy — a unified "gay agenda" — aimed at taking over American public schools and recruiting children into homosexuality. But, in actuality, the flashpoint gay issues which have emerged in schools usually arise spontaneously out of the local context.

One of the great shifts brought about by what has become known as "the Gay Mo-

The pressure of the right wing leads many teachers — gay and non-gay — to avoid dealing with gay and lesbian issues in their classrooms.

ment" — the brief period after Clinton's first inauguration when the "gays in the military" issue brought unprecedented debate and visibility to gay issues — was the vast impetus given to non-urban, non-coastal gay men and lesbians to come out and live open lives in their small towns and neighborhoods. But controversies emerge when individuals or small groups rebel against the historic silences in schools on lesbian and gay issues.

The battles usually are waged with little support from formal political and legal organizations. In this way, gay and lesbian issues in schools appear to be following a path quite distinct from that of other groups who have fought for full inclusion in schools.

Throughout the 20th century, social movements have looked to the public schools as a key institutional site for contestation. Asians and Latinos fought for equal access to education through bilingual and English-as-a-Second-Language (ESL) programs. The Civil Rights Movement spent generations fighting for school integration, culminating in the *Brown v. Board of Education* decision in 1954. The women's movement continues the fight for Title IX and the disabled community struggles aggressively for full inclusion in public school classrooms. While each population often has different histories of, and contexts for, discrimination, these movements seemed to share in a vision of public education as essential to democracy. If "their children" were to succeed in America, equal access to education had to be demanded and won.

The major national lesbian and gay organizations have not taken on public schooling as a primary site for political contestation. Other institutions such as the military and marriage have commanded the greater portion of the community's resources and political action. Only Lambda Legal Defense, the premiere gay and

lesbian legal organization, has devoted a staff position to school-related issues. Schools somehow seemed off the radar screen, despite decades of case law and the imprint of terror which remained in the memory of many gay people's minds. The central political organizations of the community focus their attention elsewhere, leaving gaps to be filled by new organizations targeting gay teachers (GLSEN) or coalitions of groups serving queer youth.

A number of organizations maintain some degree of oversight and involvement in these flashpoint battles in the schools (People for the American Way, the Human Rights Campaign, the American Civil Liberties Union, National Organization of Women). Yet only a few organizations have emerged as the leading forces combating the attacks from the right wing and offering a pro-active progressive agenda for education: the Gay, Lesbian, Straight Education Network (GLSEN), Parents and Friends of Lesbians and Gays (PFLAG), the National Gay and Lesbian Task Force, and the National Education Association (NEA) along with its local affiliates. Other groups take leadership roles on specific issues—for example, the American Library Association has fought battles to protect books with gay content from being banned in school libraries for 25 years, and the National Advocacy Coalition on Youth and Sexual Orientation is often involved in issues specifically involving queer youth.

Many have argued that the gay movement's failure to prioritize issues related to public education is rooted in two main facts. First, the movement's leaders hope to avoid providing fodder for stereotypes which portray gays as child molesters; hence, they downplay gay youth issues in the hopes of avoiding charges of "recruitment." Second, many lesbian and gay adults have failed to come to terms with their own

painful childhoods. As a result, issues facing contemporary youth are too close to home to take on. Another factor is that many leaders within the gay movement do not have children in the public schools; those lesbians and gays who work on school issues tend to be students, parents, and teachers. Taken together, these factors have caused the movement to fail to take up schools as an issue whose time has come.

One might disagree about why gay groups and left-wing organizations have failed to take a formal and significant role in fighting the right wing on gay issues in schools. Regardless, the reality is that most of the progress — on matters such as increased safety for queer youth in schools, acceptance of openly gay schoolworkers, increasing inclusion of lesbian and gay issues in school curricula — is occurring as a result of the uncoordinated and often unplanned efforts of fair-minded individuals who maintain a firm commitment to democratic education in an increasingly undemocratic era.

Behind the Classroom Door

Thus gay and lesbian youth and educators find themselves in a precarious position in the 1990s. More visible and active than ever before, they are clearer targets for an increasingly powerful right wing. Thus, the examples of school teachers actively addressing homophobia and encouraging full participation by gay parents, youth, and teachers become increasingly important as models of what can be achieved behind the classroom door.

The pressure of the right wing leads many teachers — gay and non-gay — to avoid dealing with gay and lesbian issues in their classrooms. Is it worth the risk? Teachers engage in self-censorship, sidestep sensitive questions, and participate in an elaborate "don't ask, don't tell" game with their students to keep gay issues out of the school's formal curriculum.

Some teachers have approached these issues successfully through the school's commitment to multicultural curricula — itself under attack from a right wing which insists on privileging Western cultures as the centerpiece of a narrative of universal progress. Understanding that multiculturalism might move beyond race/ethnicity to include groups defined by religion (Jews, Sikhs, Moslems) and culture (deaf people, lesbians and gays, poor people), some teachers are valiantly creating rich, radical curricula which truly aim to teach "respect for all."

Heterosexual teachers who seek to become allies with gay, lesbian, and bisexual communities might understand this work as coalition politics in its true and deeper sense. Working to support full participation in the schools might be seen as working on gay and lesbian issues. But it might also be articulated as promoting democracy and standing up to a theocratic, anti-democratic right wing. While the right consistently explains such efforts as attempts to be "politically correct" or responses to another "whiny minority group," they might more appropriately be seen as efforts to strengthen and affirm the "public" in public education. ■

Eric Rofes has a Ph.D. in Social and Cultural Studies from the University of California-Berkeley's Graduate School of Education. He is currently teaching at Bowdoin College in Maine. This article first appeared in *Rethinking Schools*, Spring 1997 (Vol. 11, No. 3).

When Schools Fail to Take Action Against Harassment
A Mother Speaks Out

The following is excerpted from remarks at a news conference in September, 1998, by the National Education Association and the Gay, Lesbian, and Straight Education Network (GLSEN). At the news conference, the GLSEN released its second annual report card on school district's policies toward gay and lesbian students and staff.

by Leslie Sadasivan

I am a nurse, a Catholic, and the mother of a gay son, Robbie Kirkland.

When my family and I realized that Robbie was gay, we let him know immediately that we loved, supported, and accepted him. After all, we had raised him to believe that God loves and accepts everyone despite their differences in race, color creed, and sexual identity. But our efforts could not protect him from the rejection and harassment he experienced.

As early as first grade, Robbie was teased and harassed because he was noticeably different from the other boys. Robbie was soft spoken, gentle, creative, and hated sports. Despite his many efforts to fit in with the other boys, such as participating in sports and pretending to have crushes on girls, Robbie was still perceived as different and eventually as gay.

When he did tell us about the early years of harassment, coming home with scratches and torn pants, of being hit by another boy in the locker room, having rocks thrown at him, and of being pushed down in the snow and called "faggot" by a schoolmate, we took him to a counselor and eventually changed his school.

Unfortunately, the teasing and harassment that so humiliated Robbie proceeded to escalate as he got older. Most of the teasing and physical attacks Robbie experienced in school occurred out of the teacher's view in hallways, playgrounds, bathrooms, locker rooms, buses, and unsupervised classrooms.

In a classroom filled with students, but no teacher, a classmate came after him with a sharpened pencil, pointed it in his face and yelled "faggot" repeatedly. Many other acts of aggression were subtle, but persistent. Over time, name calling, pushing, shoving, and general exclusion left him feeling ashamed, insecure, and alone.

It was in 8th grade that Robbie made his first suicide attempt. His suicide note began with, "Whatever you find, I'm not gay," and ended with, "Robbie Kirkland, the boy who told himself to put on a smile, shut up, and pretend you're happy. It didn't work." After that attempt, his therapist confirmed our suspicions that he was gay. Our family rallied around him. My unconditional love and acceptance blinded me from seeing how unhappy he was.

We hoped that high school would be different. Because his new high school was large, he had high hopes that he would not be picked on or singled out. But Robbie's hopes were just that, hope. Although we were not aware, the harassment continued.

Robbie shot himself in the head on Jan. 2, 1997, four months into his 9th grade year. It was the end of Christmas break. He was 14, and was found by my 19-year-old daughter Danielle. I believe his timing to be intentional so that he could avoid the pain of returning to school. Robbie wrote, " I hope I can find the peace in death that I could not find in life." He asked for us to pray for him and to remember him.

Our family has been devastated by this tragedy. Our lives are forever changed for having lost such a loving, gentle, sensitive young man. Since his death, I have told Robbie's story to whomever will listen, in the hope of bringing some good from this tragedy.

Robbie's death has already had an influence on the Catholic school which he attended. After Robbie died, the school's president addressed the student body and explicitly spelled out that gays — and indeed all people — have dignity, and that this is never to be violated. The speech will be given to all incoming freshman.

My purpose now is to help other gay youth. To this end I have become active in the gay rights movement and have joined organizations such as GLSEN and PFLAG. I sincerely hope that GLSEN's Back To School Campaign can bring about the needed change to make every school environment a safe place for gay youth. ■

A Report Card of Failure

The following is excerpted from remarks at a news conference in September 1998 by the National Education Association and the Gay, Lesbian, and Straight Education Network (GLSEN). Kevin Jennings is the executive director of GLSEN.

by Kevin Jennings

On the evening of every Labor Day for 25 years, I'd get a little nauseous. My Mom nicknamed this my "funny feeling" and I always got it on Labor Day because the next morning school would start. I got the funny feeling for the first time when I entered first grade in 1969, and was still getting it a little a quarter-century later in 1994, as I had gone "back to school" each of those years either as a student or as a high school history teacher.

My funny feeling was brought on by the anxiety I felt about going back to school—an anxiety which was not unique to me but is one to which I believe all people can relate. But my funny feeling was heightened as a teenager when I realized I was gay and when other kids started calling me faggot.

Across America this week, millions of young people had that funny feeling in their stomachs as schools reopened. For lesbian, gay, bisexual and transgendered (LGBT) students, that special anxiety raised by going back to school remains as intense as it did when I was in high school almost twenty years ago.

The results of the 1998 GLSEN Back To School Report Card are not pretty. In our survey of the nation's 42 largest districts, attended by approximately five and a half million students (or nearly 10% of all students in school in America), we have precious little evidence that school districts care at all about what happens to LGBT students. Nearly half of all districts rated received a failing grade — which meant that they do not have a single policy or program in place to protect the rights of LGBT students. Is this because there are no problems of anti-gay bigotry in our schools? Hardly. A variety of studies confirm the depth of the problem. Consider these examples:

• The Minnesota Attorney General's 1998 "Safe Schools" report cited LGBT students as the most frequent victims of harassment in the state's schools;

• The Massachusetts Department of Education reported that one in five LGBT students skips school at least once a month because they feel unsafe there (which is five times the rate of non-LGBT students);

• The Seattle public school districts found that one in six LGBT students would be attacked and physically injured so badly at some point in their high school career that they'd have to see a doctor.

When students are confronted with such harassment and bigotry, and authority figures remain silent, they learn all too well the lesson that they are literally worth less than their peers.

We're pleased that [based on their policies], eight districts have gotten A's. But we want to caution everyone not to confuse policy and practice. Schools can have wonderful policies, but if teachers and administrators do not implement them, they remain meaningless scraps of paper.

The United States was the first nation in history to create a public school system — because we believe that every child should have an equal opportunity to learn. The results of our Back To School Report Card demonstrate how far we have to go before that promise is fulfilled. Unless every district makes an explicit commitment to combat bigotry against LGBT students, we'll remain a nation where equal opportunity is something we preach but don't actually practice. Hopefully, that kind of hypocrisy gives everyone a funny feeling in the pit of their stomach this week. ∎

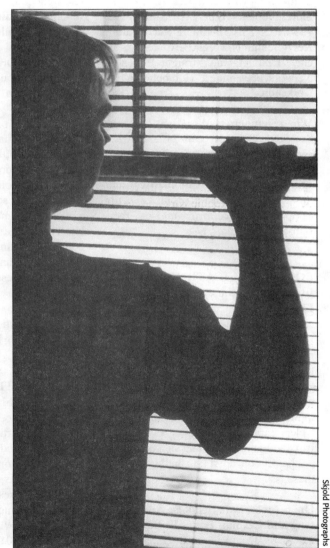

Skjold Photographs

Resources of Note

VIDEOS

It's Elementary: Talking About Gay Issues in School, Women's Educational Media, 2180 Bryant St., #203, San Francisco, CA 94110. 415-641-4616. E-mail: wemfilms@womedia.org. This astounding, 78-minute video shows elementary and middle school children discussing and participating in projects focused on lesbians and gay men. It includes candid interviews with teachers of varied sexual orientations about their classroom pedagogy on gay issues.

Teaching Respect For All, GLSEN Publications Department, 121 W. 27th St., Suite 840, New York, NY 10011. 212-727-0135. This 57-minute video features Kevin Jennings, executive director of the Gay, Lesbian, and Straight Education Network, presenting a "Homophobia 101" workshop.

When Democracy Works, by Catherine Saalfield. To order call 212-330-8220. This 30-minute video examines the radical right in the United States and links anti-gay campaigns in Colorado with anti-immigrant and anti-affirmative action campaigns in California and the racist right in Louisiana.

BOOKS/PUBLICATIONS

In the Time of the Right: Reflections on Liberation, by Suzanne Pharr. The Women's Project, 2224 Main St., Little Rock, AR 72206. 501-372-5113. A short and powerful book that presents a cogent history of the rise of the Right in the United States and offers a progressive view of the possibilities for action and social change in the current climate. The book presents a clear explanation of links between racism and homophobia and shows how the public schools are a key battleground on these issues.

Open Lives, Safe Schools: Addressing Gay and Lesbian Issues in Education, edited by Donovan Walling. Phi Delta Kappa Educational Foundation: 1996. This book offers a strong and comprehensive overview of gay and lesbian issues in public schools in the United States, focusing on professional issues, curricular matters, responses to attacks, and the needs of youth, parents, and families.

Harvard Educational Review: Special Issue on Lesbian, Gay, Bisexual and Transgender People and Education, Harvard Education Review; Gutman Library, Ste 349, 6 Appian Way, Cambridge, MA 02138. 1-800-513-0763. This special issue is an impressive volume of current research and analysis of gay issues in schools, including "A Gay-Themed Lesson in an Ethnic Literature Curriculum: Tenth Graders' Responses to 'Dear Anita,'" "Sexual Orientation and Early Childhood Education," and an interview with Cornel West on "Heterosexism and Transformation."

Gay and Lesbian Educators: Personal Freedoms, Public Constraints, by Karen Harbeck. Malden, MA: Amethyst Press: 1997. This book is the first to document the historical, social, and legal status of gay issues in American schools. Harbeck's latest book takes the reader from the early 20th century, through the McCarthy period, Anita Bryant/Briggs Initiative years, and into the present period. The volume is an extraordinary contribution to the growing literature on gay issues in education, particularly its detailed discussion of legal issues affecting teachers.

ORGANIZATIONS

The Gay, Lesbian, and Straight Education Network

GLSEN (see article p. 49) organizes local conferences and leadership training programs throughout the nation and produces videos, posters, school materials, staff development resources, and other publications. For more information, contact GLSEN, 121 W. 27th St., Suite 840, New York, NY 10011. 212-727-0135; fax # 212-727-0254.

Public Education Regarding Sexual Orientation Issues (PERSON)

PERSON produces an ongoing computer information board focused on gay issues in schools and right-wing attacks on lesbian and gay advocates. A must for organizers throughout the nation. A truly cyber-organization, they can only be reached through their web site: www.youth.org/loco/PERSONProject.

YOUTH E-MAIL LISTS

YOUTH has two lists, divided by age, to provide an outlet for gay, lesbian, bisexual, transgendered, questioning, and supportive youth ages 21 and under to talk to each other on issues such as coming out, schools, parents, friends, relationships, and other youth issues.

The lists are YOUTH 13-17 and YOUTH 17-21. (17-year-olds can subscribe to either or both lists.)

To subscribe to YOUTH 13-17, Send mail to: listproc@critpath.org. In the body of your message type: subscribe youth 13-17 [YourName, but don't include the brackets in the message].

To subscribe to YOUTH 17-21, Send mail to: listproc@critpath.org. In the body of your message type: subscribe youth 17-21 [YourName, without the brackets]. YourName can be your real name, an alias name, or your e-mail address. ■

SEXUALITY EDUCATION

Fundamentalists Successfully Pushed Stealth Legislation

Federal Law Mandates 'Abstinence-Only' Sex Ed

by Priscilla Pardini

A year and a half after federal legislation allocating $250 million for abstinence-only sexuality education, the vast majority of Americans know little, if anything, about the law. And they know even less about its potentially disastrous effects.

The legislation throws the full weight of the federal government behind programs that teach that abstinence is the "only certain way" to avoid pregnancy and sexually transmitted disease, that the expected standard of human sexual activity is "a monogamous relationship within the context of marriage," and that sex outside of marriage is likely to be "psychologically and physically harmful." States agreeing to teach abstinence can receive annual allocations of $78,526 to $4.9 million over the next five years.

Not that there's anything wrong with abstinence. In fact, if there is anything everyone agrees on when it comes to the highly charged subject of sex education, it is that abstinence is an appropriate choice for teenagers.

There's just one problem — most adolescents begin having intercourse in their mid-to-late teens, roughly eight years before they marry.

"It's not realistic to assume all teens are going to remain abstinent," said Dora Anne Mills, director of the Maine Bureau of Health. "And withholding information will not make them abstinent."

This newest controversy swirling around sexuality education in schools centers around the use of two main approaches:

• Abstinence-only curricula that teach only about abstinence. Critics say some of the most popular of these programs rely on scare tactics to get their message across and sometimes include inadequate and

inaccurate medical information.

• Comprehensive sexuality curricula that focus on abstinence but also provide teenagers with information on pregnancy, contraception and prevention of sexually transmitted diseases (STDs). Critics say such curricula increase teen sexual activity, although studies show otherwise.

As a physician and public health officer, Mills' concern about abstinence-only sex-ed programs runs deep. She points out that while reducing teen pregnancy and delaying the onset of sexual intercourse are "excellent public health goals," it is the threat of HIV and AIDS — a leading cause of death in young adults — that makes it even more critical to "give our kids the information they need to protect themselves." And with half of those who acquire HIV doing so before they reach the age of 25, Mills says it is particularly important that teenagers receive comprehensive sexuality education before graduating from high school. "In the case of HIV," she added, "withholding information can be harmful, even deadly."

According to Mills, that means delivering an abstinence message along with information on pregnancy, contraception and prevention of sexually transmitted disease. She said research has repeatedly shown that comprehensive family life education programs reduce teen pregnancy rates and delay the age at which teens first engage in sexual intercourse.

Nevertheless, programs paid for with the new federal funds must, according to law, focus "exclusively" on abstinence. That means they cannot deal with the very topics Mills and other public health officials espouse. (See interview with Joycelyn Elders on page 64.)

The federal appropriation — which balloons to $437.5 million when combined with matching state funds — is the result of a little-publicized and never-debated provision of Public Law 104-193, the welfare reform law signed into law by President Clinton in August 1996. The bill represents a big victory for its supporters — members of the religious right — who have been battling sex education in public schools for some 30 years.

The legislation, which was never the subject of public hearings or congressional debate, "took us completely by surprise," said Daniel Daley, director of public policy for the Sexuality Information and Education Council of the United States (SIECUS), a non-profit national organization that promotes comprehensive sexuality education. He said the provision was added to the legislation late in the process, when changes generally are limited to technical revisions and corrections. "An environment was created to make sure no one knew this was happening unless you were inside the loop — unless you were part of the Heritage Foundation or the Christian Coalition."

The bill, which does not require that funded programs be evaluated, was made even more powerful when it was granted entitlement status during a House-Senate conference. That means the legislation is not subject to Congress' annual appropriations process and instead automatically qualifies for funding each year of the funding period.

Attacks on Sex Ed

The abstinence-only movement began in the late 1980s in response to public support for sexuality education in public schools. (See article, "The History of Sexuality Education," page 61). It is the latest vehicle used by the religious right in its effort to impose a broad, conservative agenda on U.S. public schools. Through a series of initiatives promoting school prayer, vouchers, creationism, censorship and parental rights, conservatives have sought to impose a culture that embraces memorization and obedience at the expense of investigation, problem-solving and independent thought. The ultimate goal: to undermine the separation of church and state as it relates to public education and to bring a fundamentalist, Christian perspective to publicly-funded, secular schools.

In order to accomplish their goals, members of the religious right in the late 1980s began campaigning for — and winning — seats on local school boards across the country. The effect on sex ed has been significant. Since 1992, SIECUS' Community Advocacy Project has tracked more than 500 local controversies in 50 states around the issue of sexuality education. The following examples illustrate a number of current trends:

• School board members in Bunn, NC, ordered three chapters removed from a ninth-grade health textbook because the material did not adhere to state law mandating abstinence-only sexuality education. The chapters, covering AIDS and other sexually transmitted diseases, marriage and parenting, and contraception, were literally sliced out of the books and thrown away.

• In September 1996, by a vote of 7-2, school board members in Sheboygan, WI, virtually eliminated a sexuality education program for pupils in kindergarten through grade 3 that focused on the family and human anatomy despite strong support for the program by the district's Human Growth and Development Advisory Committee.

• A group of parents forced the Penn-Harris-Madison School District in South Bend, IN, to institute an "opt-in" policy requiring parents to provide explicit, written permission before their children can be enrolled in sex education classes. A growing trend, the move seeks to replace the standard, more workable "opt-out" policy in which parents who object to the classes must request that their children be excused from attendance.

• In March of 1994, 16 months after the religious right achieved a majority on the Vista, CA, Unified School Board, board members voted to replace a comprehensive sex-ed program with "Sex Respect: The Option of True Sexual Freedom," a fear-based, abstinence-only curriculum. When the board's attorney warned that "Sex Respect" might not meet state guidelines because it included misleading and inaccurate information, was racially biased, and supported specific religious beliefs, board members directed a new attorney to suggest modifications to the curriculum that would bring it into compliance with state law.

Abstinence-Only vs. Comprehensive Sex Ed

Although the controversy over sexuality education is being played out in a number of ways, the abstinence-only movement is clearly having the biggest impact. Abstinence-only programs are reportedly used in about 25% of the nation's roughly 16,000 school districts. Among the most popular: "Sex Respect." (See story on page 62.)

Based on fundamentalist Christian beliefs, they teach that abstinence is the only way to avoid pregnancy and sexually transmitted disease. The programs rely on fear tactics that, in effect, tell adolescents they are putting their lives at risk if they engage in premarital sex. "They tell kids they're going to go blind, get a disease, never be able to get pregnant, and ultimately die," said Monica Rodriguez, SIECUS' director of education. "That's it. That's how they get kids to be abstinent."

Experts say the approach does not work. According to the Alan Guttmacher Institute, a non-profit group that conducts reproductive health research, policy analysis and public education, teens who have participated in abstinence-only programs may be at greater risk for pregnancy and STDs once they become sexually active because they lack enough accurate information to protect themselves.

According to a 1996 report by the Institute, 56% of young women and 73% of young men have had intercourse by age 18. In response, comprehensive programs discuss abstinence in a broader context, giving youth who choose to become sexually active the information they need to protect themselves from unwanted pregnancies and sexually transmitted diseases. They also emphasize skills that kids need to truly "say no." "They learn how to get up the guts to say no, how to say it, negotiate it, stick to it," said Rodriguez.

Advocates of comprehensive sexuality education agree with Rodriguez, who says the federal government's funding of abstinence-only education is "dominating the discussion and energy around sexuality education." In Rodriguez's words, "Money talks."

Conservatives first tried, unsuccessfully, to channel federal funds to abstinence-only programs as part of an amendment to the 1994 Elementary and Secondary Education Act. They then turned their attention to health policy. By fall of 1995, language calling for $200 million in funding for abstinence-only education had been inserted in an early version of welfare reform legislation then being debated in Congress. The proposal included a detailed, restrictive definition of abstinence-only education describing it in part as any program that had "as its exclusive purpose teaching the social, psychological and health gains to be realized by abstaining from sexual activity." The proposal went nowhere, largely because of an unpopular provision that would have taken the money from existing Maternal and Child Health Block Grants.

But conservative groups did not give up and ultimately succeeded in pressuring legislators — among them former Sen. Robert Dole — to insert an abstinence-only education provision in the final version of the welfare reform bill that was passed by Congress and signed by President Clinton in late 1996. Under this provision, $50 million a year was made available to states through the Maternal and Child Health Bureau to administer abstinence-only sexuality education programs from 1998 through 2002. Programs can target children, teens and young adults, and may be administered by schools, public agencies, or community-based organizations. States must match every four federal dollars with three of their own, bringing the total amount of public money available annually to $88 million.

Daley of SIECUS traces the religious right's ultimate success to two important lessons learned from their earlier, unsuccessful attempts to legislate abstinence-only programs. "Because it's generally accepted that it's not the federal government's role to dictate [curriculum] content, they made an end run around education policy and worked through the health policy tradition," he said. "They also learned that when there's public debate on this issue, they lose. The stealth approach works."

Cleo

Deanna Duby, education director of the People for the American Way Foundation, attributed passage of the legislation to the religious right's growing Congressional power and political sophistication. "We don't have that many friends ... to stand up on the floor of Congress and say, 'I'm opposed to abstinence education.'"

All States Apply for Funds

Many states initially struggled with the decision to apply for the federal abstinence-only funds, citing the restrictive nature of the legislation, as well as the religious tone and inaccuracy of most abstinence-only programs. Also problematic for state officials is the lack of evidence that such programs delay sexual intercourse. In some cases, abstinence-only curricula conflict with existing state laws spelling out guidelines for sex ed. Another problem: coming up with matching state funds. That's no small task for a state such as New York, which will have to find $2,533,188 in state money in order to qualify for a total of $3,377,584 in federal funds in 1998.

Yet despite the drawbacks, every state in the union and the District of Columbia applied for federal money. "Clearly, many felt political pressure to do so," said Daley. "Who wants to be painted as not being supportive of abstinence for young people?"

The money looks particularly good to perpetually cash-strapped local school districts that see the abstinence-only legislation as a lucrative source of new dollars over the next five years. Daley said districts saw the funds as "budget relief" — money that could be used to purchase curricula such as "Sex Respect" that meet the federal definition of abstinence and free up resources previously spent for comprehensive sex-ed programs. "It's the path of least resistance — an easy, cheap way to save young people," he said. "Unfortunately, life is much more complicated."

Stan Kocos, regional director of the AIDS Resource Center of Wisconsin, predicted that efforts to reconcile the use of abstinence-only curricula paid for with federal dollars in states where such programs are deemed inappropriate — and perhaps illegal — was going to create "mass confusion." He said creating confusion — in part by throwing out "as much misinformation as possible so that it's difficult to examine" — ultimately would work to the advantage of those who want to narrow the curriculum. "School districts capitulate to get out from under the constant controversy," he said. "You can only get pounded on so much before you say 'This isn't worth it anymore.'"

Best Case Scenario

If there's any good news on the abstinence-only front, it centers around valiant efforts in many states to find ways to use the new federal dollars for non-school-based, public health programs that supplement rather than replace existing comprehensive sexuality education programs.

Some examples: after-school, off-campus counseling and mentoring programs that provide at-risk youth with remedial education, career advice and adult supervision; programs that focus on preventing drug and alcohol abuse, which increases teens' vulnerability to sexual advances; and programs that help teens deal with depression, which can lead to acting out sexually. In other cases, states will target younger teens — especially those under 14 — for whom the abstinence-only message is particularly appropriate and who are most likely to take it seriously.

Some states, including Maine, are using their money for public service media campaigns reinforcing the message that abstinence is an appropriate choice. Mills, the director of the Maine Bureau of Health, said her office was planning a series of 60-second TV spots discussing the deadliness of HIV, the importance of parent-child communication, and the fact that "dating is more than hitting a home run and scoring." She said the ads would deliver important messages while also counterbalancing today's "sex-saturated" television programming.

But even as public health officials scramble to come up with responsible programs that qualify for the federal abstinence-only money, the religious right is trying to scuttle such efforts, which they say do not adhere closely enough to the letter of the abstinence-only law. The National Coalition for Abstinence Education, a far-right coalition of 45 mostly state-level groups, for example, is "grading" state strategies for promoting abstinence under the law. States that use their money for classroom programs focusing on the eight tenets of the federal definition of abstinence receive high grades. States that run media campaigns, target younger students, and run mentoring programs, receive "Fs." Oklahoma and Louisiana are two states that have been forced to revise their plans because of low grades from NCAE.

Given such a climate, Daley and other advocates of comprehensive sexuality education often feel they are fighting a losing battle. Daley likens the abstinence-only funds to "hush money, so adults don't have to worry about what's happening to young people." The legislation perpetuates the illusion, he said, "that if we just tell kids to say 'no,' and to respect marriage between heterosexuals, all our problems will be solved."

"What we couldn't do with half a billion dollars over the next five years and the cooperation of the nation's governors," Daley continued. "That's what's so disheartening. Five years will go by, and comprehensive programs that show promise will not have been funded. And that's where we'll be at the beginning of the new millennium." ■

Priscilla Pardini is a Milwaukee-based writer specializing in educational issues. This article first appeared in *Rethinking Schools*, Summer 1998 (Vol. 12, No. 4).

The History of Sexuality Education

The 1960s saw the beginning of the current wave of controversy over sex ed in U.S. schools. But as early as 1912, the National Education Association called for teacher training programs in sexuality education.

In 1940, the U.S. Public Health Service strongly advocated sexuality education in the schools, labeling it an "urgent need." In 1953, the American School Health Association launched a nationwide program in family life education. Two years later, the American Medical Association, in conjunction with the NEA, published five pamphlets that were commonly referred to as "the sex education series" for schools.

Support for sexuality education among public health officials and educators did not sway opponents, however. And for the last 30 years, battles have raged between conservatives and health advocates over the merits — and format — of sexuality education in public schools.

The first wave of organized opposition, from the late 1960s to the early 1980s, took the form of attacks aimed at barring any form of sex ed in school. Sex education programs were described by the Christian Crusade and other conservative groups as "smut" and "raw sex." The John Birch Society termed the effort to teach about sexuality "a filthy Communist plot." Phyllis Schlafly, leader of the far-right Eagle Forum, argued that sexuality education resulted in an increase in sexual activity among teens.

Efforts to curtail sex ed enjoyed only limited success, however. Sex education programs in public schools proliferated, in large part due to newly emerging evidence that such programs didn't promote sex but in fact helped delay sexual activity and reduce teen pregnancy rates.

By 1983, sexuality education was being taught within the context of more comprehensive family life education programs or human growth and development courses. Such an approach emphasized not only reproduction, but also the importance of self-esteem, responsibility, and decision making. The new courses covered not only contraception, but also topics such as family finances and parenting skills.

In the mid 1980s, the AIDS epidemic irrevocably changed sexuality education. In 1986, U.S. Surgeon General C. Everett Koop issued a report calling for comprehensive AIDS and sexuality education in public schools, beginning as early as the third grade. "There is now no doubt that we need sex education in schools and that it [should] include information on heterosexual and homosexual relationships," Koop wrote in his report. "The need is critical and the price of neglect is high."

But if Koop's report helped promote sexuality education, it also forced the Religious Right to rethink its opposition strategies. Even the most conservative of sex-ed opponents now found it difficult to justify a total ban on the topic. Instead, the Right responded with a new tactic: fear-based, abstinence-only sexuality education. ■

— Priscilla Pardini

A Look at the "Sex Respect" Curriculum

Consider the story of "LaWanda," a homely teenager being raised by a single mother who is pressured by her more sexually experienced boyfriend, "Calvin," into having sex. Soon after, Calvin dumps LaWanda and takes up with another girl.

"LaWanda was torn apart by the pain of being left alone by the men in her life, first her father and now Calvin," continues the story. "How would she ever be able to trust another man again?"

Meanwhile, teenagers with names like "Chris" and "Cindy" help each other say no to sex.

Welcome to "Sex Respect," the most popular of the abstinence-only sexuality education curricula, where racial bias and gender stereotyping are just two ways of getting teens to "Just say 'No'" to sex.

The story of "LaWanda" and "Calvin" reinforces a number of negative stereotypes, according to "Sex, Lies, and Politics," a 1997 report on abstinence-only curricula in California Public Schools, by the Public Media Center and the Applied Research Center in Oakland. According to the report, these stereotypes include:

"that African Americans are promiscuous; that African-American men are uncaring, unfaithful and irresponsible; and that African-American women have grown up in troubled homes, aren't physically attractive, and need male attention for self-esteem."

"Sex Respect" also "teaches students to fear their sexuality, reinforces gender stereotypes, and delivers misinformation on, and discourages use of, condoms and other contraceptives," according to the report. In addition, the curriculum, "framed by a religious bias of moral absolutism...uses misinformation about AIDS/HIV to reinforce an anti-gay bias, and encourages those who have sexually 'transgressed' to embrace 'secondary virginity.'"

Some examples from the text:

• A fear- and shame-based approach: "There is no way to have premarital sex without hurting someone," states one lesson. Another message: "Sex before marriage ... a quick way to lose at the game of life." And what of teens who attempt to protect themselves from pregnancy or sexually transmitted diseases by using contraception? "You feel guilty beforehand because now you are 'planning' to do something wrong for you, and you can't pretend anymore that 'it just happened.'"

• Inadequate and inaccurate medical information: Premarital sex is equated with increased incidence of cervical cancer. The failure rate of condoms is exaggerated. AIDS is inaccurately described as "the STD most common among homosexuals and bisexuals." The curriculum also says, "Our nation's laws, which are designed to protect the health of its citizens, require a blood test before couples can get their marriage license. This test will tell you if you or your intended spouse is carrying an STD." In fact, laws vary by state and the blood test referred to is for syphilis only, not all STDs.

• Homophobic bias: Homosexuality is mentioned only in connection with a lesson on AIDS, thereby equating it with disease. AIDS is also called nature's way of "making some kind of a comment on sexual behavior." ■

Cleo

SEX, etc.
A Newsletter by and for Teens

José and Diane saw their chance.

Diane's parents were away for the weekend. The two had been dating for five whole weeks and they were ready.

So on Saturday night, José showed up, with no condom in his pocket, but with an idea of what was going to happen. And it did.

At age 17, Diane and José both lost their virginity. A few days later, they broke up. Diane's mom found out what went down and laid down the law — no more José. He was crushed.

"I thought sex would make our relationship stronger," says José, now 19 and a whole lot smarter. "But it didn't work out that way. I really regret it."

So begins an article in the latest edition of *Sex, etc.*, a newsletter on sexuality written for teens and by teens. In the story, by Angel Alamo, a senior at Camden High School in Camden, NJ, teens talk about the first time they had sex.

Alamo said the teens he interviewed for the story had no qualms about talking with him about such an intimate subject. "I did the interviews over the phone, and I told them we didn't have to use their real names," Alamo said. "I think they were comfortable talking to me."

The only publication of its kind, *Sex, etc.* is a frank, sexually explicit newsletter published three times a year by the Network for Family Life Education, a coalition of public, private, and nonprofit agencies that supports family life education — including comprehensive sexuality education — in school and community settings. The network is housed in the Rutgers University School of Social Work in New Brunswick, NJ.

The eight-page newsletter, aimed at high school students, is distributed free — with a discussion guide — to 400,000 teens in 49 states. It is used in schools and teen centers and by city health departments, and is shipped to doctors' offices, hospitals, juvenile detention centers, and other community-based organizations serving youth. Its cost is underwritten by foundations, corporations, and state government grants. Last May, the National Campaign to Prevent Teen Pregnancy recognized the impact of *Sex, etc.* at an awards dinner in Washington, DC.

Articles in the newsletter cover a wide range of subjects, including: abstinence, contraception, teen parenthood, sexually transmitted disease, AIDS, gay and lesbian teens, sexual harassment and violence, abortion, substance abuse, and child sexual abuse. In addition to Alamo's article, the latest edition of *Sex, etc.* carried stories titled "Am I My Partner's Keeper?" on pregnancy prevention; "A Painful Lesson: Anyone Can Get Herpes," on ways to prevent sexually transmitted diseases; a question-and-answer column featuring an interview with author Dr. Ruth Westheimer; and stories on teens and alcohol.

Nancy Parello, an AP reporter who acts as newsletter coordinator, said the key to *Sex, etc.* is that kind of balance. "We try to cover everything from every angle," Parello said. "The kids write about abstinence — that there are good things about waiting. But we recognize that there are kids out there who are having sex, and that we need to speak to them as well."

Parello, who edits the newsletter, recruits teens from across New Jersey to serve on the newsletter's editorial board. Board members take part in two days of training on public health issues and journalism, and then meet eight Saturdays throughout the year with Parello to discuss issues related to teen sexuality, brainstorm story ideas, line up sources, and critique each other's stories. Every story is reviewed for medical accuracy by Ann Schurmann, the Network's program manager and a health educator who holds a master's degree from Columbia University's School of Public Health. When appropriate, story content is also reviewed by physicians and other health experts.

But the newsletter's biggest draw is that it is written by teens for their peers. Most articles include interviews with teens who tell of their own sex-related experiences. "I know lots of teenagers who can't talk to their parents about sex or go to their teachers," said Anupama Mehta, 17, a senior at Old Bridge High School in Old Bridge, NJ. "For them, this is the only way to get good information. I wanted to be part of that process."

Both Alamo and Mehta said it was important to approach the highly intimate subjects they write about with a high degree of professionalism and maturity. "The issue of STDs is very, very personal," said Mehta, who wrote a story on genital warts for a recent edition of the newsletter. "But I can't be afraid to ask questions that might be embarrassing. I have to ask. It's very important to get this information out."

Parello said she continues to be amazed by the serious, straightforward way the teenagers approach their subject matter and sources. "You get a lot more snickering and giggling going on when adults talk to kids about sex," she said. "When kids talk to kids, it's not as embarrassing. They're really listening to each other." ■

An Interview with Joycelyn Elders

'Vows of Abstinence Break More Easily than Latex Condoms'

The following is condensed from an interview with former U.S. Surgeon General Joycelyn M. Elders. A pediatric endocrinologist, the 64-year-old Elders is on the staff of Children's Hospital in Little Rock, Arkansas, and on the faculty of the School of Medicine at the University of Arkansas. She was interviewed by Priscilla Pardini.

What's wrong with abstinence-only sexuality education programs?

Nothing, in the very early grades. If we did a really good job in the first 10 or 12 years of children's lives teaching them about abstinence, as well as about honesty and integrity and responsibility and how to make good decisions, we would not have to be talking to them at 15 about not getting engaged in sex.

But we haven't done that. Mothers have been teaching abstinence, schools have been teaching abstinence, preachers have been preaching abstinence for years. Yet more than three million teens get STDs every year, and we still have the highest teen pregnancy, abortion, and birth rates in the industrialized world. But we seem to feel that we don't need to educate our children about their sexuality. That makes absolutely no sense. We all know the vows of abstinence break far more easily than latex condoms.

Teens need a comprehensive sexuality program that gives them all the information they need to become empowered and responsible for preventing pregnancy and disease. We have to stop trying to legislate morals and instead teach responsibility. Abstinence-only does not do that. You can't be responsible if you don't have the information.

Isn't sexuality education better left to parents?

I have no problem leaving it to parents, if you have parents who can and will do it. But we have many dysfunctional parents — some on drugs, some into alcohol, some who are stressed out, and some who just don't know how to talk to their children about sex. Then the responsibility belongs to the community. And since the only place we've got access to every child is in school, we need to use our schools to teach about sexuality. We don't depend on parents to teach math and English and science and geography. So why should we depend on parents to teach children all of their social and behavioral skills?

Doesn't sexuality education cut into precious time now allotted to basics such as reading and math?

I think teachers are doing a wonderful job — the best they can under difficult circumstances. But what good is knowing math and science if you don't know how to protect yourself? The fact is, we invest more money in prisons than we do in schools. We're putting out a dragnet when we ought to be putting out a safety net.

Our children, from the time they enter kindergarten through 12th grade, spend 18,000 hours watching TV, but only 12,000 hours in reading and math classes and only 46 hours in health education classes. I say let's take away some of the TV time — and devote more hours to the school day, to summer school.

How early should sexuality education start? What kinds of topics should be covered in the early years?

As early as kindergarten children need to be taught to respect their bodies, to eat in healthy ways and to feel good about themselves. They need to know how to make good decisions and how to deal with conflict in non-violent ways. People who feel good about themselves feel in control of their lives and can make decisions that are right for them. Years later, these children, if they choose to be sexually active, will probably also choose to use a latex condom to protect themselves. But if you're not in control of your sexuality, you can't control your life. Those are the people who end up saying, "It just happened."

How can teachers evaluate whether material is age-appropriate for their students?

There are a lot of high-quality, well-tested curricula out there that are age-appropriate. Even very young kids should know that anytime anyone touches you in a way you don't want to be touched, even if it is your parents, you have to tell

> *Teens need a comprehensive sexuality program that gives them the information they need to become empowered and responsible for preventing pregnancy and disease. We have to stop trying to legislate morals.*

somebody. That message needs to start in kindergarten, but also needs to be repeated and reinforced.

Older kids should learn about the menstrual cycle, that if they choose to be sexually active they can get diseases or get pregnant. They should know that you can get pregnant the first time you have sex ... that you can get pregnant if you have sex standing up.

By high school, you need to be teaching them more about responsibility and equality — that boys and girls have equal responsibility for their sexuality. They should be taught about date rape, about birth control. They should be taught to assume that anytime they have sex they are risking — boys and girls — AIDS, sexually transmitted disease, and becoming a parent. At this point, when you simply tell them they should "just say no," they look out the window and start singing. It's too little too late.

> *We need to use our schools to teach about sexuality. We don't depend on parents to teach math and English and science and geography. So why should we depend on parents to teach children all of their social and behavioral skills?*

What about the charge that teaching teens about sexuality actually increases sexual activity?

There has never, never been any study that has documented that teaching young people about sex increases sexual activity, and most studies say it decreases sexual activity. In fact, according to a new study ["Impact of High School Condom Availability Program on Sexual Attitudes and Behaviors," *Family Planning Perspectives*, March-April, 1998] even when condoms were made available in a high school, sexual activity did not increase.

How serious are teen pregnancy, STDs and HIV among teens?

There are more than 3 million STDs a year reported in those under 19 years of age. Genital herpes — which cannot be cured — has increased almost 30% in young people in the last eight or nine years. The pregnancy rate is slightly down, but there are still almost 900,000 teen

Kirk Anderson

pregnancies a year. When it comes to HIV, the largest increase in cases is seen in teenagers. This is serious. The stakes are very high.

Sex education has been part of the curriculum in many schools for many years. Why isn't it working?

We've not had comprehensive K-12 sexuality education. We're still out there giving kids an annual AIDS lecture. We might as well keep that. We don't teach math by giving one lecture a year. You have to do it all the time and keep reinforcing it. We're not making a committed effort to change things. What we're doing is criticizing and blaming. The problem is, we're willing to sacrifice our children to preserve our Victorian attitudes. We know what to do. We know how to do it. We just don't have the will to get it done.

In the 1960s, when we found out our children were behind in math and science, we added courses in math and science. So if we want to address the social problems our children are having now, we have to put in the programs to do it.

How should a school administrator respond if a parent or group of parents demands that an abstinence-only curriculum be taught?

A superintendent should agree with the parents and put in an abstinence-only program for kindergarten and elementary students. When it comes to older students, he really needs to tell other parents what's going on so they can rise up and fight. Ultimately, a superintendent has to do what his board members tell him to do. But it's the parents who carry the big stick. Parents can get anything they want, and two major studies have shown that most parents want comprehensive sexuality education, with condom availability, in the schools. Yet, because of their silence, they let this other side get their way and destroy their children.

What is the relationship between public health departments, public schools,

In fact, according to a new study, even when condoms were made available in a high school, sexual activity did not increase.

and the U.S. Surgeon General's office?

There should be a marriage between schools and public health. We should have health education programs in schools along with school-based clinics that would be easily accessible to students and affordable. Now, many young people don't know where to go or don't have the money to pay for health services. We also need to teach people how to be healthy. We have a health-illiterate society, and one place to correct that is in the schools. I think the Surgeon General has a role to play in promoting good health practices and focusing on prevention — to try and make this country as healthy as it can be. ■

This interview first appeared in *Rethinking Schools*, Summer 1998 (Vol. 12, No. 4).

Resources on Sexuality Education

Sexuality Information and Education Council of the United States, 130 W. 42nd. St., New York, NY 10036-7802. 212-819-9770; fax 212-819-9776. e-mail: siecus@siecus.org. Internet address: www.siecus.org. Promotes comprehensive education about sexuality, provides resources, and advocates the rights of individuals to make responsible choices.

Planned Parenthood Federation of America, 810 Seventh Ave., New York, NY 10019. 212-541-7800; fax 212-245-1845. e-mail: communications@ppfa.org. Internet: www.plannedparenthood.org. They provide technical assistance to local communities working in support of comprehensive sexuality education.

National Abortion and Reproductive Rights Action League, 1156 15th St. NW, Suite 700, Washington, DC 20005. 202-973-3000; fax: 202-973-3096. e-mail: naral@naral.org. Internet: www.naral.org. NARAL conducts legal and policy research, public education campaigns, and leadership training. Its mission calls for promoting policies, such as sexuality education, that make abortion less necessary. NARAL's 1995 "Sexuality Education in America: A State-by-State Review," was the first national survey of sex education laws.

Network for Family Life Education, Rutgers University, 100 Joyce Kilmer Ave., Piscataway, NJ 08854. 732-445-

7929; fax 732-445-4154. Contact them via e-mail: netfle@rci.rutgers.edu. The Network for Family Life Education is a coalition of public, private, and nonprofit agencies that support family life education, including comprehensive instruction about human sexuality. Its publications include "Family Life Matters," a newsletter for educators, social agency staff, and policy-makers, and "Sex, etc.," a health and sexuality newsletter written by teens for teens. Back issues of "Sex, etc." can be accessed on a web site, designed by teens, that also gives visitors a chance to ask questions that will be answered by "Sex, etc." experts. Internet address: www.rci.rutgers.edu/~sxetc. ■

VOUCHERS

NAACP Warns of the Dangers of Vouchers

No Child Should Be Left Behind

by Kweisi Mfume

In this richest and most powerful nation on earth, we at the NAACP believe that no child should be left behind. America's children deserve the best education we can provide them.

In 1998, we find ourselves facing an issue that is in some ways the old familiar fight for fairness, but we must instead regard it as a new fight demanding our vigorous attention. The attacks of the right on our children's future have solidified around a concept of exclusion and selective opportunity called "vouchers."

As I've said before, the extreme ultra-conservative policies of the far right wing in our nation are Draconian, punitive and backward. They are policies that punish the elderly, restrict the poor and deny opportunity to our children. These policies that threaten our American ideals must be countered with effective and realistic responses that reflect our need as a society for inclusion and tolerance.

Vouchers are one of these threats.

The National Association for the Advancement of Colored People is proud to join with the People for the American Way Foundation in taking a stand against this terrible threat. No other scheme poses a greater danger to the idea that no

child should be left behind.

Voucher proposals take many forms, and some are designed to deliberately disguise the basic realities that will result over time. The best students will be skimmed off — those whom private schools find desirable for their own reasons. Since families will have to make up additional costs, those in the upper-and middle-income brackets will be helped the most — as long as their kids don't have personal, behavioral or educational

challenges that cause the private school to pass them by.

The surest losers are the poorest children with the most urgent need for a good school system. Many of them would not be able to afford the extra tuition, transportation and related costs of using a voucher. Many of those who could afford such costs would never be accepted to selective private schools anyway.

Skin color, religion, economic class, language group, need for remedial work — all these things would be barriers to acceptance and success in a system designed around the choices of private schools, not the choices of parents and students.

But we are a people of hope and determination. We have opportunity in concept beyond what we've know before; but history has taught us that freedom is a constant struggle. We are not surprised to

---

The attacks of the Right on our children's future have solidified around a concept of exclusion and selective opportunity called "vouchers."

---

discover that the fight must continue if we are to make opportunity and equality real for all children.

Education must be a fundamental guarantee for each child, and for our nation's precious democracy. The struggle for educational opportunity for all our children remains at risk. Regrettably, the opposition is gathering strength. They are packaging the threat to that opportunity attractively and spending millions to make it policy.

Once again, we are being called upon to stand up on behalf of our children and to fight back. We are determined to turn back the efforts of the right to gain additional political power and economic gain for their private interests using votes and tax dollars that belong to all our children.

As we prepare to cross over into a new millennium of hope and challenge, we at the NAACP believe that no child should be left behind. ■

Kweisi Mfume is president and CEO of the NAACP. The above is excerpted from "Partners for Public Education," a joint publication of the NAACP and People for the American Way Foundation.

Jean-Claude LeJeune

10 Reasons To Oppose Vouchers

Vouchers are the centerpiece of the conservative agenda to privatize education and substitute the marketplace for our system of democratically controlled schools. Following are "talking points" that summarize arguments against vouchers.

Vouchers are about privatization, not opportunity. They are about reducing government responsibility for safeguarding the good of all.

1. Vouchers are a diversion.

Vouchers take time and energy away from needed reforms that can improve our public schools. "Choice" sounds nice in theory but does nothing to address more pressing problems such as class size, teacher training, out-dated and over-crowded buildings, and inadequate funding systems that allow many suburban systems to spend twice as much per pupil as urban and rural schools.

2. Vouchers are taxation without representation.

Vouchers funnel public dollars to private schools, yet taxpayers have absolutely no say in how voucher schools are run. Further, private schools are not required to meet basic accountability standards, such as open meetings and records law, or to make public their employees' wages and benefits, the number of dropouts, their standardized test scores, and so forth. Private schools are called "private" for a reason — they don't have to answer to the public at large.

3. Vouchers are based on the marketplace, not the public good.

Vouchers rest on the assumption that the marketplace holds the answer to complicated educational and social problems. This assumption has proven false in so many other key areas, such as health care, housing, and jobs. Ultimately, a marketplace approach always favors those with more money and resources. Should that be our vision for public education?

4. Vouchers stand in opposition to this country's democratic vision.

Our founding fathers understood that education is an essential prerequisite for full participation in society. Vouchers foster narrow self-interest, individual choice, and an escape mentality. Yet democracy, at its heart, is about working together for what is best for all children.

5. Vouchers violate the separation of church and state.

At a time when world events from Bosnia to India to the Middle East underscore the importance of church/state separation, it is more important than ever that we abide by the constitutional safeguards that have guided this country for more than 200 years.

6. Vouchers are about privatization, not opportunity.

Vouchers, the top conservative education goal, are at the heart of the right-wing attack on the public good. The conservative agenda looks with disdain upon public institutions. Ultimately, it seeks to reduce government responsibility for safeguarding the good of all — while maximizing government support for private and corporate gain.

7. Vouchers will siphon money off from financially strapped public schools.

Politicians are not talking about using vouchers to increase the amount of money devoted to education reform. They are merely shifting money from public schools to private schools.

8. Voucher schools will cream off "desirable" students and leave those they don't want for the public schools.

In particular, private schools tend not to provide needed services for children with special educational needs or for children who speak English as a second language. It's the private school that chooses the student, not the other way around.

9. Vouchers schools will increase segregation.

The first vouchers schools in this country were specifically set up to allow white students to flee integrated schools in the South. In Milwaukee, as in many urban areas, private schools tend to be highly segregated and are used by some white parents to avoid desegregation efforts. Desegregation is not a panacea to our public schools' educational problems. But do we want to return to the Jim Crow philosophy of "separate but equal?"

10. Private schools do not have to respect the constitutional rights of students.

Private schools, by their very nature, are shielded from guaranteeing students the rights to due process and freedom of speech given to students in public schools. Students have fewer rights, not more, in private schools. Will this also be true for private school receiving vouchers?

Earlier in this century, education pioneer John Dewey argued for a strong public school system as essential to democracy. As policy-makers confront the issue of vouchers, it would be prudent to listen to Dewey's warning:

"What the best and wisest parent wants for his own child, that must the community want for all its children. Any other ideal for our schools is narrow and unlovely; acted upon, it destroys our democracy."

■

— Barbara Miner

Questions and Answers About School Choice

by the Editors
of *Rethinking Schools*

SCHOOL CHOICE

Kirk Anderson

When people talk about school "choice" what do they mean?

People generally are talking about voucher plans that would allow tax dollars to be used for tuition at private schools, including religious schools. Choice is also used sometimes to refer to proposals that let students attend public schools in other districts, or that allow students to choose various public schools within a district.

Are there many voucher initiatives in the United States?

There are two programs providing public dollars for private voucher schools: in Milwaukee and Cleveland. Both provide money for low-income children to attend

voucher schools located within city boundaries. Both also include religious schools, which raise concerns about the separation of church and state. The legality of the programs will ultimately be decided by the U.S. Supreme Court.

On a national level, Republican legislators have also spearheaded efforts to institute various tax schemes — such as tuition tax credits or tax-free savings accounts for education — that would provide public dollars for private schools. In a number of cities and states, there are also privately funded initiatives to provide partial tuition for children to attend private schools. By and large, these private measures are designed to build political support for publicly funded vouchers.

There have been four efforts to use referenda to demand statewide voucher programs: in Oregon, California, Colorado, and Washington state. All four efforts defeated by a margin of roughly 2-1.

Historically, voucher plans were instituted in some southern states in an effort to circumvent the *Brown* decision outlawing segregated, "separate but equal" school. These plans were declared unconstitutional by the U.S. Supreme Court.

On a national level, vouchers have become the dominant theme of the conservative movement's education agenda.

Vouchers would give more parents the

opportunity to send their children to a private school. What's wrong with that?

Parents and students must have choices. Few would disagree with that. Nor is anyone criticizing the right to a privately funded education. But when it comes to public schools, limiting one's concern to the rights of individual parents fails to do justice to the complexities of public education in a democratic society.

Freedom is more than an individual concern. It also involves safeguarding the democratic freedoms of society as a whole and providing equal educational opportunities for all children.

It's impossible to think about public education without understanding its relationship to democracy. Schools are the place in this society where children from a

---

Freedom is more than an individual concern. It also involves safeguarding the democratic freedoms of society as a whole. It's impossible to think about public education without understanding its relationship to this country's democratic vision.

---

variety of backgrounds come together and, at least in theory, learn to talk, play, and work together. Schools are by no means equal and play a significant role in maintaining our highly stratified society. At the same time, there is no comparable arena in this country where there is a vision of equality — no matter how much this vision may be tarnished in practice — and where people of different backgrounds interact on a daily basis. Certainly it doesn't happen in our highly segregated neighborhoods. Nor does it happen in the workplace, where there's no pretense that people come together as equals. Nor does it happen in our churches.

It was clear to early thinkers like Thomas Jefferson that education was a public responsibility that was essential to creating and sustaining a democracy. In a truly democratic society, citizens have to be trained to rule. Public schools are integral not only to preparing children to be full participants in society but to be full participants in this country's tenuous experi-

ment in democracy. We seem to have lost that vision.

But don't parents have a right to choose a school that they feel coincides with their value system, even if it's a private school?

Parents have the right to choose any school they want — but they don't have the right to expect that the taxpayer will pay for that school. Further, it's not simply a matter of parents choosing a private school but of private schools choosing students. And the school's choice always wins. If a private school doesn't want your child, whether for academic, disciplinary, religious, or financial reasons, there's nothing you can do.

The more important issue is that parents — and taxpayers — have not only the right but the responsibility to become involved in the public schools. And this needs to take place in the broader context of fighting for a better education for all kids.

The possibility for democratic discussion of what is best for all our children would virtually disappear under a voucher system.

What is so bad about opening up the voucher program to religious schools?

The core issue is that individuals would be paying tax money to support schools with religious values that might be antagonistic to their own religious values. Religion is a profoundly private matter and should remain that way.

Vouchers force taxpayers to fund religious schools that may disturb deeply held principles. Should Jewish taxpayers be forced to fund Christian schools with anti-Semitic beliefs? Should gay and lesbian taxpayers have to pay for religious schools that believe homosexuality is a sin?

Wouldn't vouchers allow lower-income families to send their kids to private schools and get a better education. Isn't it a move toward more equality?

In the long run, abandoning public education will only increase inequalities in education. Some low-income families might benefit from voucher plans, but most poor people would still go to public schools — and these schools would have fewer resources because taxpayers' money would be going into private schools. Further, many proponents of vouchers believe vouchers are the magic bullet of school reform — and as a result criticize other needed reforms such as smaller classes or equitable funding of schools in urban, rural and suburban areas,

If policy-makers who promote vouchers really want to further equity, they should consider vouchers in the range of $10,300 — the median tuition at private high schools in the National Association of Independent Schools. And they would force private schools to accept all students who apply, based on a lottery system. But there's no voucher plan anywhere in the country that offers such money or adequately safeguards against discrimination.

Furthermore, there's no data to support claims that private schools are automatically better than public schools. In particular, there is little data on private elementary schools. Unlike public schools, private schools are under no requirement to release information on test scores, expulsions, drop-outs, attendance, and so forth.

Because public schools are a monopoly, they don't have to worry about competition. Wouldn't vouchers force public schools to be more innovative?

Voucher supporters often shout the accusation "monopoly" but ignore the highly decentralized nature of American education. There are over 15,000 school districts in this country and they vary significantly in demographics, tax bases, governance, and curriculum. Most education decisions are made at the district level. Unlike in other industrialized countries, the federal government in the United States plays a modest role in education.

Certainly, competition can spark creativity, and in good public schools teachers compete amicably to better serve students. But competition can also create social disasters — just look at the effects of corporate down-sizing, or the competition in the health insurance industry to reduce medical costs and increase profits.

It's also important to remember that competition in business depends heavily on advertising and cutting costs. Do we really want our schools to follow the lead of business and cut costs to the bone, perhaps by getting rid of "extras" such as libraries or music and art rooms? Or mimic corporate advertising, by spending precious dollars on public relations efforts?

Bureaucracy acts like a sledgehammer and beats the life out of schools. Wouldn't vouchers help break this bureaucracy?

We must reduce bureaucracy in our schools, and developments toward decentralized control of schools are healthy steps in that direction.

But we can't make bureaucracy into a scapegoat for all our problems. There are good schools within large, bureaucratic school systems, and there are bad private schools that are free of bureaucratic oversight. In some cases, bureaucratic regulations are hard-won protections helping to guarantee equity around bilingual education, affirmative action, and education for the physically challenged. It would be a step backward if such regulations were thrown out or ignored.

Unions are some of the strongest opponents of private school vouchers, because they fear losing their power and membership. Isn't the union position self-serving?

Unions have the right to oppose attempts to turn services over to non-union workers. Given the attacks on unions in recent years, both by the government and by businesses, teacher unions have legitimate fears.

Undoubtedly, some union officials and teachers have lost sight of what is in the best interests of children. But many teachers honestly question whether the marketplace will magically lead to quality. They work passionately to improve schools and worry what will happen when the seats are filled up in the private schools and there are still millions of children left to attend a public school system depleted of resources.

Why has the idea of vouchers become so popular?

First, there is legitimate dissatisfaction with the failures of the public schools. In urban areas, in particular, far too many schools are failing our children.

Most important, however, there has been a conservative counterrevolution against public services generally. The solution to society's problems is posed in terms of the marketplace, and privatization plans are cropping up all over. Getting rid of our system of public education would be the final coup in the conservative attempt to reduce the role of government in providing social services for the good of all.

Third, we have to consider whether there is a relationship between the willingness to abandon urban schools and the fact that the leadership and student population of urban schools are increasingly people of color.

Fourth, it's important to look at how businesses and wealthier individuals can directly profit from privatizing education. Middle-class parents who are already sending their children to private schools, for example, will get government aid to help pay the tuition. Also, some businesses hope to make money by setting up private schools or getting contracts for different educational services.

What's your alternative vision for improving the schools?

There's no one simple answer, but one can outline the elements of meaningful reform. We must reorganize our schools so parents and teachers have more say. We must overhaul our curriculum to promote critical thinking and a multicultural perspective. We must demand racial and gender equity. We must eliminate tracking. We must change our testing and assessment so we assess thinking and learning, not just how well one answers multiple choice questions out of context. We must improve the quality of teacher training and have smaller class sizes. On a state level we should equalize funding for school districts. On a federal level, we need to substantially increase our funding for education.

There never has been, nor ever will be, a system where everyone is able to choose a school that perfectly fits their needs. The only viable solution is to improve the entire system of public education so that parents aren't forced to compete for a few select schools. ∎

Rick Reinhard

The Market Is Not the Answer

**An interview with
Jonathan Kozol**

We've got to be blunt about the problems in public schools. But we can't succumb to the nonsense that a public system is inherently flawed and so we have to turn to the marketplace.

The very word "public" has a negative connotation these days. How does one counter that negative image in a way that one can defend public schools but not defend the status quo?

We've got to be blunt about the problems in a public system and be harsh critics of those problems. We don't want to be in the position of knee-jerk defenders of the public schools against the bad guys.

But we have to be careful not to succumb to this nonsense that a public system is inherently flawed and that therefore we have to turn to the market place for solutions. I've never in my entire life seen any evidence that the competitive free market, unrestricted, without a strong counterpoise within the public sector, will ever dispense decent medical care, sanitation, transportation, or education to the people. It's as simple as that.

I think it's time for us to begin to look back at some of our roots as Americans. It's absolutely crucial to claim the high moral ground on this issue and make it clear that the right-wing voucher advocates are subverting a strong American tradition. In this respect, we are the defenders of American history.

Let me state it differently. The complaints about the apparent malfunction of the public system are linked, in my belief, to the peculiar problems of impoverished, often virtually colonized, urban school systems. I mean "colonized" in the sense that very little power actually exists within the system, least of all the most important power which is finance, for which they're dependent on outside forces. And those outside forces are the people who set tax rates, the state government, the federal government, and the people who shape economic policy in America. I don't think the problems in urban public schools are inherently those of public education. I see hundreds of fine suburban school systems all around the country where nobody ever raises any question about the dangers of monopoly, because these are well-funded, reasonably attractive school systems.

Monopoly Not the Problem

I think it's important to recognize that this issue of monopoly never came up until people realized the incredible problems of our segregated, impoverished, colonized inner city systems, and needed to find a scapegoat other than segregation and colonization. The issue to me is not that these are public institutions. The issue is that these city schools are basically powerless. The superintendent is usually the viceroy representing other interests to which the superintendent has to be deferential, usually at great emotional cost.

My own faith leads me to defend the genuinely ethical purposes of public education as a terrific American tradition, and to point to what it's done at its best — not simply for the very rich, but for the average American citizen. We need to place the voucher advocates, the enemies of public schools, where they belong: in the position of those who are subverting something decent in America. ■

Jonathan Kozol is the author of Savage Inequalities, Amazing Grace, *and other books on children.*

SCHOOL ~~VOUCHERS~~ *VULTURES*

Lessons of Chile's Voucher Reform Movement

by Martin Carnoy

Voucher plans have been in place for many years in other countries. Contrary to the claims of pro-voucher advocates in the United States, the experience internationally suggests that voucher plans promise a lot but may actually be worse for children from low-income families, for whom the gains are supposed to be the greatest.

"The primary negative effect of school choice is its natural tendency to increase the educational gap between the privileged and the underprivileged," John Ambler, referring to voucher plans in Britain, France, and the Netherlands, wrote in the *Journal of Policy Analysis and Management* (1994).

The most interesting comparison is from Chile, which has a long-standing voucher plan where pupils have been assessed regularly. The Chilean plan began in 1980 under the Pinochet military government as part of an overall "de-governmentalization" free-market package. It meets almost all the conditions of those in the United States who advocate "choice with equity," including fully subsidized, deregulated private schools competing head-on for pupils with deregulated municipality-run public schools in all metropolitan neighborhoods, from middle-class suburbs to low-income barrios.

One key feature of the Chilean plan was privatizing teacher contracts and eliminating the teachers' union as a bargaining unit. Teachers were transferred from the public employee system to the private sector. By 1983, even public schools, meaning those schools run by municipalities, could hire and fire teachers without regard to tenure or a union contract, just like any un-unionized private company. Another feature was to release all schools from the previously strictly-defined structure of the national curriculum and from national standards.

What were the results of this reform?

Result #1: Spending Drops

The first result was that even when parents' contributions are included, total spending on education fell quite sharply after increasing in the early 1980s when the central government was paying thousands of teachers severance pay as part of privatizing their contracts. In 1985, the federal contribution was 80% of total educational spending, and total spending was 5.3% of Gross National Product (GNP). Five years later, the federal portion was 68% of the total, and the total had fallen to 3.7% of GNP. Private spending rose, but not quickly enough to offset the drop in real federal contributions.

Result #2: Increased Stratification

The second result was that in Chile, as in Europe, those who took advantage of the subsidized private schools were predominantly middle- and higher-income families.

Chile offers a voucher to all students. "Fees" often are charged at the private schools on top of the voucher, and private schools are allowed to screen students. (There are also elite private schools which do not take part in the voucher plan, where students' families pay the complete tuition.) As a result of the voucher reform, there was a massive shift of students into private schools, in particular middle-class and upper-middle-class children. By 1990, of families in the lower 40% of the income distribution, 72% attended municipal public schools. In the next highest 40% income bracket, only 51% of the families sent their children to public schools, with 43% in subsidized private schools and 6% in elite private schools where parents paid the full tuition. And in the top 20% income bracket, only 25% had their children in public schools, with 32% in subsidized private schools and 43% in elite private schools.

Result #3: No Academic Improvement

The third result was that the increase in pupil achievement predicted by voucher proponents appears to have never occurred.

Scores in Spanish and mathematics from two nationally standardized cognitive achievement tests implemented in 1982 and 1988 for fourth graders registered a national decline of 14% and 6%, respectively. According to World Bank economist Juan Prawda, the test scores fell most for low-income students in public schools, but they also fell for low-income students in subsidized private schools. Middle-income students had small increases in test scores whether they were in public or subsidized private schools. Subsequent tests in 1990 showed increases of 9% in Spanish and 11% in math, but this still left scores about the same as in 1982. Middle-income students averaged higher scores on these tests in private schools than in public, but lowest-income students tended to do better in public schools. University of Georgia political scientist Taryn Rounds' estimates of pupil achievement as a function of type of school, location, parents education, and students' socio-economic class using the 1990 test results confirm that lower-social-class students did better in public schools on both the Spanish and math tests, and middle-class students did better in subsidized private schools.

Because low-income parents were less able to add private contributions to the voucher amounts, private schools in Chile were apparently not that interested in doing any better than public schools with lower-income pupils. If the declining scores in Chile's municipal public schools mean anything, it is that increased competition had a negative effect on student achievement, and that the Chilean voucher plan contributed to greater inequality in pupil achievement without improving the overall quality of education.

Some analysts in Chile claim that subsidized private schools cost less because they have somewhat higher pupil-teacher ratios and pay their teachers lower salaries. But there is no evidence that this means that private schools are becoming more "efficient." Indeed, if private schools are consistently "creaming off" easier-to-teach students, municipal schools may have to maintain smaller classes with more highly paid teachers just to stay even academically.

Result #4: Need to Re-Centralize

The fourth result was the need to recentralize influence over the educational system once a democratic government was elected in 1990. Under the Pinochet reform, government made no effort to improve the curriculum, the quality of teaching, or the management of education, since this was supposed to happen spontaneously through increased competition among schools vying for students. It did not. Neither did municipalities or most private schools come up with incentives for improving pupil performance. Low-income municipalities were at a special disadvantage because they, even more than other municipalities, lacked the fiscal capacity and resources for school improvement. And as soon as unions were legal again, teachers reorganized themselves, fought for higher salaries, and for the right to representation. Not surprisingly, they focused their demands on the central government, which oversees minimum salaries for both public and private schools.

Lessons for the United States

The lessons for us here in the United States are obvious, but they are not the one that privatization advocates want

known. Voucher plans increase inequality without making schools better. Even more significantly, privatization reduces the public effort to improve schooling since it relies on the free market to increase achievement. But the increase never occurs. Private schools may end up producing higher achievement than public schools, but they generally do this by keeping out hard-to-manage pupils, who get concentrated in "last-resort" public schools.

There is another lesson to learn from the Chilean case. At the end of the voucher road, the case for public schools becomes more, not less, difficult. The new democratically elected government, which by U.S. standards would be considered center/left, continues to blame public school bureaucracy and lack of market incentives for the low level of achievement in municipal schools. Once a voucher plan is implemented, many middle-class parents find that they like their children being separated from low-income students. Furthermore, teachers in public schools find that given the worsening conditions and lack of support, it is even more difficult to be innovative. This last lesson should spur public school advocates to support rapid and radical reforms of schools in inner cities now, and to emulate, sooner rather than later, those

reforms that seem to be working for at-risk students.

Chile had a military dictatorship in the 1970s and 1980s that could impose vouchers from above and suppress opposition by force. In a democracy, it takes highly dissatisfied constituencies to produce reforms, even if they are not the ones who ultimately benefit from them. Conservatives have figured out that the most dissatisfied educational constituencies are the poor, and will use them to dismantle public education.

Ironically, the privatization movement in the United States is gaining ground just when pupils from all groups, especially those most at risk, are making significant achievement gains and just when public school reform movements are reaching into inner cities to produce real change. To cite one example: between 1975 and 1989, the difference in average reading proficiency scores between African-American and white 17-year-olds went from 50 points to 21 points, or a gain of about half a standard deviation.

The best antidote to vouchers is to spread public school reform — fast. ■

Martin Carnoy is a professor of education and economics at Stanford University. This article is adapted from an essay that originally appeared in *Education Week*.

Public Dollars for Private Schools: A Pandora's Box

by Barbara Miner

Tenasha Taylor, an African-American student at an elite private high school, learned the hard way that private schools get to operate by different rules than public schools.

Taylor gave a speech on Black separatism in her English class at University School of Milwaukee. She also criticized the school as racist. Suspended and asked not to return to the school the following fall, Taylor sued on grounds of free speech. She lost.

In his opinion, Federal Judge Terrence Evans wrote, "It is an elementary principle of constitutional law that the protections afforded by the Bill of Rights do not apply to private actors such as the University School. Generally, restrictions on constitutional rights that would be protected at a public high school ... need not be honored at a private high school."

Taylor's 1995 case has taken on new implications following the Wisconsin Supreme Court's decision this summer upholding the constitutionality of Milwaukee's program that provides vouchers to private and religious schools.

It's not mere coincidence that the term "private" is so often followed by the phrase, "Keep Out!" Private schools, like private roads and private country clubs, don't have to answer to the public. That's why they are called "private."

What does it mean when private schools get public dollars yet don't have to follow the same rules as public schools? The answer is particularly crucial in Milwaukee because 100% of a private school's students can be funded by vouchers — in other words, the school doesn't have to have a single student who privately pays tuition — and the school still gets to call itself "private" and operate accordingly.

Under Milwaukee's program, voucher schools:

Jean-Claude Lejeune

• Do not have to obey the state's open meetings and records laws.

• Do not have to hire certified teachers — or even require a college degree.

• Do not have to release information on employee wages or benefits.

• Do not have to administer the statewide tests required of public schools.

• Do not have to publicly release data such as test scores, attendance figures, or suspension and drop-out rates. The only requirement is a "financial and performance evaluation audit" of the entire voucher program to be submitted to the legislature in the year 2000.

One of the fiercest controversies has erupted over special education students, who account for about 15% of Milwaukee public school students. The voucher schools argue that, even when such students are enrolled in a private school (which the schools help ensure doesn't happen too often), it is up to the public schools to provide any special services such students may need.

There's also the issue that some white parents in Milwaukee have used private schools to get around desegregation. The Milwaukee public schools, for instance, are approximately 60% African American. At some of the most popular Catholic high schools, only 3% to 5% of the students are African American.

The voucher schools also balked at a letter from Wisconsin's Department of Public Instruction (DPI) this summer asking that the schools comply with federal and state protections on issues such as free speech, due process, and non-discrimination based on gender, marital status, pregnancy, and sexual orientation. (The only legislative requirement is that they not discriminate on the basis of race, color, or national origin. The school are also to accept voucher students on a random basis.)

The legal issues are particularly complicated because religious schools can receive vouchers. Under the First Amendment, the government is not to "entangle" itself in the running of religious institutions. Thus religious schools can legally fire teachers who violate the schools' views on religious principles — such as a gay teacher or a teacher who supports the right to abortion. Will religious schools that receive vouchers also be able to teach that homosexuality is a sin, that creationism is superior to the theory of evolution, that the Jews killed Christ?

The Milwaukee offices of the American Civil Liberties Union and the NAACP, meanwhile, have initiated a campaign to

> *It's not mere coincidence that the term "private" is so often followed by the phrase, "Keep Out!" Private schools, like private roads and private country clubs, don't have to answer to the public.*

alert parents and students of their rights. The groups argue that the law, as interpreted by the courts and the Department of Public Instruction, calls upon voucher schools to respect a broad range of rights. "When tax dollars go to private institutions, taxpayers as well as parents deserve to know that those tax dollars will not support discrimination," said Chris Ahmuty, executive director of the ACLU of Wisconsin.

The voucher schools argue that they should not be governed by the same rules that apply to public schools. As Dan McKinley, a leading spokesperson for the Milwaukee voucher schools, told *The Milwaukee Journal Sentinel:* "These schools are clearly not public schools."

As with many issues in the Milwaukee voucher program, the controversy is sure to land in the courts. ∎

Voucher Resources

Following are some of the most prominent national organizations providing information on vouchers.

American Civil Liberties Union. The ACLU has been active in pointing out the dangers of vouchers to the First Amendment. It has also played a leading role in protecting students' rights. *Contact:* 125 Broad St., 18th floor, New York, NY 10004. 212-549-2500. E-mail: aclu@org. Internet: www.aclu.org. Be sure to also check out the Wisconsin ACLU web page: www.acluwisc@execpc.com.

American Federation of Teachers. The AFT has a range of material on vouchers and privatization, in particular on for-profit schools. *Contact:* Dan Murphy, Office of the President, AFT, 555 New Jersey Ave., NW, Washington, DC 20001. 202-393-6325. Internet: www.aft.org.

Americans for Religious Liberty. This group has an extensive publications list on the religious right and on issues such as vouchers. *Contact:* Box 6656, Silver Spring, MD 20916. 301-598-2447.

Americans United For Separation of Church and State. Americans United focuses on First Amendment issues, in particular on the voucher movement. *Contact:* 1816 Jefferson Place, NW, Washing-

ton, DC 20036. 202-466-3234.

National Association for the Advancement of Colored People. The NAACP has launched a Partners for Public Education campaign in conjunction with People for the American Way Foundation. *Contact:* 4805 Mt. Hope Dr, Baltimore, MD 21215. 410-358-8900. Internet: www.naacp.org.

National Committee for Public Education and Religious Liberty (PEARL). PEARL is particularly involved in litigation and has a broad range of materials. *Contact:* PO Box 586, FDR Station, New York, NY 10150. 212-486-4590.

National Education Association, Center for the Advancement of Public Education (CAPE). The center has a variety of information and resources on vouchers, privatization, and for-profit education companies such as The Edison Project. *Contact:* NEA, CAPE 1201 16th St., NW, Washington, DC 20036. 202-822-7446. Internet: www.nea.org.

National PTA. The PTA has launched a joint initiative with the National Association of School Boards to push Congress to support public schools and to vote no on vouchers. Contact them to get their "Protect America's Public Schools: An Action Kit to Stop Vouchers." *Contact:* National

PTA, 330 N. Wabash Ave., Suite 2100, Chicago, IL 60611. 312-670-6782. Internet: www.pta.org. E-mail: info@pta.org.

People for the American Way Foundation. It is probably the best single source of information on vouchers and on the religious right. It also helped launch the national African American Ministers Leadership Council, which is involved in grassroots organizing against vouchers. *Contact:* 2000 "M" St., NW, Suite 400, Washington, DC 20036. 202-467-4999. E-mail: pfaw@pfaw.org. Internet: www.pfaw.org.

Public Research Associates. PRA has a broad range of materials on the right wing. *Contact:* 120 Beacon Street, Suite 202, Sommerville, MA 02143. 781-661-9313 Internet: www. publiceye.org.

* * *

Rethinking Schools has available an 88-page booklet, *Selling Out Our Schools: Vouchers, Markets, and the Future of Public Education.* We also have a section on vouchers in *Rethinking Schools Online,* at www.rethinkingschools.org. We regularly report on voucher-related issues in our quarterly *Rethinking Schools* (subscription is $12.50 per year). For more information call our office at 1-800-669-4192. ∎

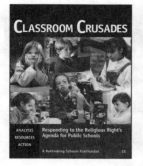

ORDER FORM

Name _____

Address _____

City _____ State _____ Zip _____

Phone(day) _____ Phone(eve) _____

E-mail _____

Method of payment

❏ Check or Money Order made out to
   Rethinking Schools
❏ Purchase Order
❏ MasterCard   ❏ Visa

   Credit Card Number:

   _____

   Expiration Date: _____
   Authorized Signature:

   _____

Mail to:

**RETHINKING SCHOOLS
1001 E. Keefe Ave.
Milwaukee, WI 53212**

**414-964-9646
FAX: 414-964-7220
E-mail: RSBusiness@aol.com**

Toll-free: 1-800-669-4192

*Shipping and Handling
U.S. shipping and handling costs are 10% of the
total. Minimum S&H charge of $3.50.
Canadian shipping and handling costs are 25% of
the total. Minimum S&H charge of $4.50.
For orders outside the United States or Canada,
contact our office for shipping costs.

Bulk orders of special publications are for
schools and school districts, or for internal
use by organizations. They are not to be sold
publicly or resold for profit. Book stores and
distributors call for trade discounts.

Books/Booklets

Classroom Crusades

___ Number of copies x $_____ (Unit price) $_____

Funding for Justice

___ Number of copies x $_____ (Unit price) $_____

Selling Out Our Schools

___ Number of copies x $_____ (Unit price) $_____

Rethinking Our Classrooms

___ Number of copies x $_____ (Unit price) $_____

Rethinking Columbus

___ Number of copies x $_____ (Unit price) $_____

Books/Booklets Subtotal $ _____

Shipping and Handling* $ _____
USA: 10% of subtotal (Minimum $3.50)
Canada: 25% of subtotal (Minimum $4.50)

Subscriptions

❏ Two-year subscription: $20.00 $_____
   (Save $5.00)
❏ One-year subscription: $12.50 $_____

   Subscriptions to Canada and Mexico,
   add $5.00 per year. $_____

   All other international subscriptions,
   add $10.00 per year. $_____
❏ Sample copy: $3.50 $_____
❏ Send me information about reduced
   bulk subscription rates.

Subscription Subtotal $ _____

TOTAL ENCLOSED $